The Assassination of the Black Male Image

by Earl Ofari Hutchinson, Ph.D.

MIDDLE PASSAGE PRESS
Los Angeles, CA

Publisher
MIDDLE PASSAGE PRESS
5517 Secrest Drive
Los Angeles, CA 90043-2029
(213) 298-0266

Printed and bound in the United States.
Publisher's Cataloging in Publication
(Prepared by Quality Books, Inc.)

Hutchinson, Earl.
    The assassination of the Black male image / Earl Ofari
Hutchinson.
    p. cm.
    Includes bibliographical references and index.
    Preassigned LCCN: 93-080991
    ISBN 1-881032-11-6.
    1. Afro-American men--Social conditions. 2. Afro-American
men--Psychology. 3. Sex role--United States. 4. Man-woman
relationships. 5. Afro-American parents. I. Title.

E185.86.H87 1994   305.38'8960'73
                                                    QBI94-172

ACKNOWLEDGEMENTS

Special thanks to Matt Blair, Rene Childress and, of course, my wife BBH for bouncing my sometimes crooked ideas back to me on a straight line.

*To those who have kept the faith of our fathers,
when others haven't.*

CONTENTS

Aunt Sally: "What's kep' you?—boat get aground?"

Huck: "Yes'm—she—"

Aunt Sally: "Don't say yes'm—say Aunt Sally. Where'd she get aground?

Huck: I didn't know what to say because I didn't know whether the boat would be coming up the river or down. Now I struck an idea, and fetched it out: "It warn't the grounding—that didn't keep us back but a little. We blowed out a sylinder head."

Aunt Sally: "Good gracious! anybody hurt?"

Huck: "No'm killed a nigger."

Aunt Sally: "Well, it's lucky; because sometimes people do get hurt."

Mark Twain, *The Adventures of Huckleberry Finn* (WW Norton: New York, 1977), p. 174-175.

OVERVIEW

The Growth Industry in Black Male Mythology

I have a confession to make. Author Terry McMillan was holding forth on stage in the main reading room at the San Francisco Book Festival in 1992 and I didn't know who she was. From the rapturous gaze on the faces of the several hundred women in the main reading room, I knew she was important. Many of them tightly clutched copies of her monster best seller *Waiting to Exhale* to their breasts. I had vaguely heard that the book loosely dealt with four black women who sift through a motley bunch of losers and deadbeats trying to find a "good black man." One reviewer called it "a tough love letter" for black men.

This made me uneasy. I edged closer to the stage to listen. As she read excerpts from the book, she waved her hands, cocked her wrist defiantly on her hips, frowned, pouted and laughed. The crowd loved every minute of it.

During the question and answer period, several dozen women scrambled to the floor mikes. Terry snapped out answers firmly and with authority. Then, someone asked the inevitable question," What did black men think of the book?" Terry didn't miss a beat. "Yeah," she huffed, "they didn't like it, but that's their problem." They laughed and applauded.

Toward the end, a young black woman asked her if she planned to write a sequel to the book. Terry paused for a moment, laughed and said, "No, the women are all married and happy now." The questioner glided away with her copy locked in a death grip and with a heavenly glow on her face. The audience laughed and applauded.

I didn't. Her answer gnawed in my gut and wouldn't let loose. Later, when I read *Waiting to Exhale*, I knew why. Three of the suffering four women, Gloria, Bernadine and Robin in their rage called black men: ugly, stupid, prisoners, unemployed, crackheads, short, liars, unreliable, irresponsible, possessive, old and set in their ways. They weren't talking about the black men they dated, screwed and loved. They weren't talking about the men they heard their friends, relatives, acquaintances, mother and maybe even grandmothers talk about. They weren't talking about the men they read about in books or saw on TV. They were talking about ALL BLACK MEN!

If the four black women were now happily married, they must have found black men who were handsome, intelligent, not convicts, employed, drug-free, tall, truthful, dependable, sharing, sexually exhilerating, mature and flexible.

Why didn't Terry want to tell the world about them? Did she think nobody cared about them? Did she believe that Black America is, as *Newsweek* claimed, "A World Without Fathers." Did she believe one or more of the stereotypes that black men are criminals, derelict, lazy, violence prone and sexually irresponsible dregs? If she did, I wouldn't be surprised.

II

The image of the malevolent black male is based on a durable and time-resistant bedrock of myths, half truths and lies. The image was created during the European conquest of Africa, nurtured during slavery, artfully refined during the nadir of segregation, and revived during the Ronald Reagan-George Bush years. I'm not picking on sister Terry. Many have profited handsomely from the lucrative growth industry America has fashioned out of black male bashing.

To maintain power and control, the plantation masters said that black men were savage and hyper-sexual. To strengthen racial control, late Nineteenth and early Twentieth Century scientists and academics concocted pseudo-theories that said black men were criminal and mentally defective. To justify lynching and political domination, the politicians and business leaders of the era said that black men were rapists and brutes. To roll back civil rights and slash social programs, Reagan-Rush Limbaugh type conservatives say black men are derelict and lazy.

To secure big Hollywood contracts and media stardom, the young black filmmakers say the "boyz in the hood" are gangbangers, drive-by shooters and dope dealers. To hustle mega record deals and concert bookings, the rappers and comedians say black men are "niggers" and more incredibly, "bitches." To nail down book contracts and TV talk show appearances, black feminist writers say black men are sexist exploiters.

The corporate controlled media defiantly drops the words

"racism" and "economic injustice" from its vocabulary. It pounds, twists and slants all of these stereotypes into sensational headlines and sound bites, and dumps them back on the public as fact.

A black man can be wealthy, possess status, be politically and socially connected and still wind up on the image assassin's list. The glitter and glamour of the entertainment world couldn't save Michael Jackson or Spike Lee. The fan adulation and mega contracts in the sports world couldn't save Michael Jordan or Mike Tyson. The rarefied atmosphere of politics couldn't save Marion Barry or Clarence Thomas. The social activism of the black freedom movement couldn't save Martin Luther King, Jr., Malcolm X, Marcus Garvey, Paul Robeson or W.E.B. DuBois.

III

What about black women? Aren't they victims too? Of course, many black women are poor, raped, battered, abused, called "bitches" and "hos" and stuck with bills and babies. Terry was right, some black men do these things to black women.

But America has not made the black woman its universal bogeyman. The black man is. Here's four reasons why I say that. First, I'm a black man. I hear, see and feel the pain of black men daily. Second, I can count. For a black man, here's the grim picture: He will live, on average, to be sixty-seven years old. She will live to be seventy-three years old. He's one- and one-half times more likely than her to drop dead of a heart attack. He will have a far greater death rate from cancer, stroke, pneumonia, and AIDS than she will.

Then there are the unnatural causes of death. Compared to her, he's five times more likely to kill himself by his own hand, three times more likely to be killed in a car accident, and four times more likely to be killed by someone else. Meanwhile, one out of four young black males languish in prison, on parole or probation. One out of seven will be murdered. One out of three black males are unemployed.

Third, I know America's dirty little secret. Many white men hate and fear black men. Yet they are fascinated with them. They love to see them sing, dance, lug and toss those balls. In deeply sexist America, the game is still about white male ego and power. Black men are perceived as threats to both.

Fourth, black women are black and poorer. But they're still women. Most white men don't need to wage the same ego war against her as they do against black men. They occasionally depict her as a woman always burdened and eternally suffering. They tell her that she wouldn't be in the mess she's in if HE would just get a job, stay out of jail, stop shooting or snorting up, get married, stop making babies and quit dropping dead so fast (for some not fast enough).

The plot to assassinate the black male image has deep roots in America's sinister racial past. To understand the complexity of the plot and the circle of conspirators, we'll start with the era when many white Americans dropped the code words, skipped the niceties and called the black man what they truly thought he was, a beast.

1

The Negro a Beast . . . or in the Image of God

I wish Rodney King would read Charles Carroll's *The Negro a Beast or in the Image of God.* He might understand why many white folks said rotten things about him. This is what I mean. In November 1992, King spoke to about seventy-five students at Tustin High School in the mostly white southern California suburban bedroom community of Orange County. This was King's first major public appearance in nearly a year. King, being a modest unassuming man, had purposely kept a low profile.

It didn't help. People still bad-mouthed him. They called him a doper, an alcoholic and a violence-prone ex-convict. Many openly grumbled that King himself had provoked the cops. Some even smirked and whispered that he deserved the ass-whipping. In the Simi Valley trial of the four LAPD cops who beat King, defense attorneys in a bravura performance used this sneaky racism to their advantage and got them off. One unnamed juror said of King, "He was obviously a dangerous person, massive size and threatening actions."

King and his attorney Milton Grimes were fed up with this kind of talk. They figured that high school students would be sympathetic. King, himself a high school dropout, would benignly tell the kids to stay in school. They hoped this would improve his image.

It didn't. The following day, angry readers deluged the *Los Angeles Times* with calls objecting to school officials letting "a dangerous, parolee" on a high school campus. The Tustin High School principal felt the heat, back-pedaled fast and claimed it was all a mistake. Sounding properly indignant, he agreed that King was not a suitable "role model."

II

He was "dangerous," of "massive size," "threatening," and "a poor role model." Remember those words as I turn back the pages of history a century and more. Carroll said that and much more about black men in his grotesque little book published in 1900. Reading the passages of his book even without the filter of America's hideous racial past, one might have reason to laugh.

Carroll, however, was dead serious. His book was not published by the Ku Klux Klan in rural Mississippi or Alabama, but by the American Book and Bible House in St. Louis. The book was a brisk seller. Carroll argued that the black man was left out of human creation and was a subspecies of the animal world.

Carroll was not a quack. He did not make any of this up. He considered himself a man of pure science. He based his "theory" on the meticulous research of Alexander Winchell a distinguished professor of geology and paleontology at the University of Michigan. When the evidence got a little skimpy in some places, Carroll retreated into scripture. He swore that God warned that since creation the world's troubles began when human beings let the Negro "beast" mingle among them.

Carroll had his critics. Georgia theologian W.S. Armstead was indignant that he would dare bring the word of God into this. By calling black men beasts, he felt Carroll was letting them off the hook. Armstead said the black man was a cunning, calculating degenerate who followed his "murderous heart" and brutally "waylaid" white women.

Armstead didn't have much chance against learned men like Carroll and Winchell. They were Northerners and for nearly a half century they had beaten the South to the punch every time when it came to propagating myths about black bestiality.

George Fitzhugh, a Virginia newspaperman, sometime planter and always articulate defender of slavery was delighted to find that his Northern brethren were very receptive to his views. In 1854, Fitzhugh, in *Sociology for the South*, wrote that "slavery rescued blacks from idolatry and cannibalism, and every brutal vice and crime that can disgrace humanity."

Fitzhugh took his act on the road and headed North. He quickly discovered that many influential power brokers thought that his *Sociology for the South* should be the sociology for the North. Many leading newspapermen quoted him. Businessmen wined and dined him. Some Northern congressman snipped quotes from his writings and placed them into the *Congressional Globe* (later *Record*).

During the Civil War, dozens of Northern newspaper editors and politicians were livid because Old Abe and his Republican political cronies had the audacity to shed white blood to free black savages. At every turn, they raised the bloody flag and tried to sabotage the war effort.

III

The Civil War ended legal slavery, but it did not put the old planters entirely out of business. They still had one big trump card to play: The Black Scare. They played it hard by convincing whites, North and South, that blacks were out to get land, power and white women. Soon men in white sheets silhouetted the night sky with their fiery crosses. Their terror campaign to whip the black beasts back in line was a smashing success.

Reconstruction was dead. The abolitionists who had pricked the conscience of the nation were too old and tired to care anymore. The ranks of the Radicals in Congress were thinning by the hour. And, Northern whites were dead set against risking their necks to fight for the rights of men who they didn't really believe were men.

Meantime, the learned men of the North like Carroll were busy mangling science to shape the image of the black man as criminal, sex crazed, violent and degenerate. Dr. Frank Hoffman, in 1896, backed Carroll to the hilt. Hoffman like Carroll was not a Southerner. In fact, he was not a Northerner. In fact, he was not even an American. Hoffman, writing from Germany, declared that there was such an "immense amount of immorality and crime" among black men it had to be part of their "race traits and tendencies."

The message to worried whites: sit back, relax and let nature take its course. All those decadent black men would soon die out from their own "inferior organs and constitutional weaknesses." Hoffman's wise words were rushed into print by the prestigious American Economic

Association (AEA).

Another learned Northerner, Walter F. Wilcox, chief statistician for the U.S. Census Bureau, thought the good doctor had the right ZEITGEIST. Three years later with the blessing of the American Social Science Association, Wilcox pinned up his charts, juggled figures and solemnly predicted that blacks were "several times" more likely to commit crime than whites. He wasn't finished. The next year he told the social scientists that Hoffman was right. Blacks were doomed to go the way of the Dodo Bird and Dinosaur because of "disease, vice and profound discouragement."

The American Economic Association was on a fast track to get the official words of its scholars out to the public. They rushed Historian Paul Tillinghast's paper on "The Negro in Africa and America" into print. Tillinghast agreed with the other scholars. He cautioned them not to forget that blacks were "seriously handicapped by the inherited conditions" they brought with them from savage Africa.

Around the same time, Dr. G. Stanley Hall was determined not to be outdone by the AEA. The president of the American Psychological Association and founder of the *American Journal of Psychology* thought his fellow academics were putting too much emphasis on "race traits." As a clinician, he believed there were murky forces at work in the black psyche. According to his diagnosis, the black man's "disthesis, both psychic and physical is erethic, volatile, changeable, prone to transcoidal, intensely emotional and even epileptoid states." Buried somewhere between the "erethic" and "transcoidal," gibberish was a hopeless dimwit. The public should be on the alert.

A soon to be president didn't dispute this. In 1901, Virginia University Professor Woodrow Wilson in the *Atlantic Monthly* asked what could one really expect of individuals who were really little more than a "host of dusky children" "insolent and aggressive, sick of work, covetous of pleasure."

The line-up of highbrow intellectual magazines that endorsed this gobbledygook read like a roll call of academia. They included, *Popular Science Monthly, The Annals of the American Academy of Political and Social Science, Medicine* and *the North American Review.* They all chimed in with volumes of heady research papers, articles and scholarly opinions that "proved" blacks were hopelessly inferior, crime and violence-prone defectives from which society had to be protected.

IV

Since art does imitate life, it was only a matter of time before this pap crept into the literature. At first, Northern and Southern novelists did not lay it on too thick. The blacks in their stories were mostly grinning, buck-dancing, lazy, slightly larcenous darkies. As the scientists kept up their drumbeat warnings about the black menace, the novelists soon turned vicious. Upton Sinclair had impeccable credentials as a Socialist crusader. Still, in his popular muckraking novel, *The Jungle,* published in 1905, Sinclair was appalled that white girls working in Chicago's hellish stock yards rubbed shoulders "with big black buck Negroes with daggers in their boots."

This was too tame for Thomas Nelson Page. He wasn't a man of subtlety when it came to racial matters. But, first, he had to lay the proper groundwork. In an essay, *The Negro: The Southerner's Problem,"* he warned that the old time darkies were dying off and that the "new issue" was "lazy, thriftless, intemperate, insolent, dishonest and without the most rudimentary elements of morality." In his novel, *Red Rock,* he continued to warn of the dangers of the black peril.

Thomas Dixon, Jr. wasn't satisfied with this. Page only talked about the "new issue" Negro. Dixon set out to vanquish him. In his big, sprawling novel, *The Clansman,* published in 1905, Dixon described him as "half child, half animal, the sport of impulse, whim and conceit...a being who left to his will, roams at night and sleeps in the day, whose speech knows no word of love, whose passions once aroused, are as the fury of the tiger." It sent collective chills up the spines of much of white America. Bolt the doors. Turn out the lights. Praise the Lord and pass the ammunition. The black beast was coming. In *The Clansman,* Dixon had the right men to defend society, and (white womanhood) from this creature, the Ku Klux Klan.

Dixon knew he was on to something big. When *The Clansman* was adapted for the stage, it brought down theater houses everywhere. Audiences were delirious. They had to see the KKK destroy the black beasts. Soon Broadway's great white way picked up on Dixon and made him the toast of New York. *Theater IV,* the trendy magazine of the *haute art* crowd, gave him a free platform to explain "Why I Wrote *The Clansman.*" Dixon swore that he wasn't a bigot that it was based on "historical authenticity." *The New York Evening Post* was impressed. It praised him for tackling "a question of tremendously vital importance."

Filmmaker D.W. Griffith wanted Americans to know just how important it was. A decade later, he turned *The Clansman* into *Birth of a Nation.* He brushed off vehement protests from the NAACP and black leaders that it was all a lie. He could afford to. By then cash registers were jingling everywhere as the film smashed house records nationally. When the film hit the White House, an ecstatic Woodrow Wilson exclaimed, "It's like writing history with lightening." Griffith wasn't the only filmmaker who sniffed dollars and glory in foisting the black brute's criminal image on the public. Between 1910-1911, these gems graced the screen, *Rastus in Zululand, Rastus and Chicken, Pickaninnies and Watermelon* and the *Chicken Thief.*

NOTE: I always thought it appropriate that these parts were played by white actors in messy cream black face. I knew then who the real toms, coons, mulattos, mammies and bucks were.

By then, there were many whites who didn't need to read Dixon's novel, or see Griffith's film to know what to do with the "half child, half animal." The year *The Clansman* was published, more than one black person was lynched, burned, shot or mutilated every week in America. The year Griffith's film debuted the weekly lynch toll was still the same.

The NAACP's W.E.B. DuBois bitterly called lynching America's "exciting form of sport." Page was undaunted. He chalked lynching up to the "determination to put an end to the ravishing of their women by an inferior race."

NOTE: Many people still think that black men were lynched because they committed rape. They weren't. In most cases, they weren't even accused of rape. Even then, the apologists for "the sport" knew this. I'll have more, much more to say on this later.

V

Politicians, being politicians, seemed to feel that if the public believed that black men were inherent rapists then why spoil it with the truth. So, when Teddy Roosevelt rose to address Congress in 1906, lynching was very much on his mind. He sternly lectured that, "The greatest existing cause of lynching is the perpetration, especially by black men, of the hideous crime of rape."

The old Rough Rider didn't want anyone to get the idea that he was condoning lynching, after all, it would look a little odd for the man sworn to uphold the law to applaud those who broke it. He obligingly denounced the "lawbreakers." But Teddy had made his point. The *Cincinnati Inquirer* in 1911 railed against black men for committing the "unspeakable crime" and bragged that "the mob is the highest testimony to the civilization and enlightenment and moral character of the people."

The *Inquirer* was not a lone voice. The press, always on the lookout for a sensational story, read the public mood. In the crimson days before the doughboys of World War I marched off to save the world for democracy, the press milked the black beast angle for all it was worth. The *New York Times, Chicago Tribune, Boston Evening Transcript, San Francisco Examiner, Atlantic Monthly* and *Harpers* heisted the lingo from the academics and had great fun ridiculing, lampooning, butchering and assailing black men in articles and cartoons. They were "brutes," "savages," "imbeciles," "moral degenerates," and always "lazy, lazy, lazy." *Century Magazine* claimed it overheard this exchange between two blacks:

Uncle Rastus: "Now dat you daddy too ole to work, why don yah get a job?

Young Rastus: No! indeed ain't going to have folks say everybody works but father 'bout mah family."

Remember Uncle Rastus was a good ole darkie. The young one, well......

The San Francisco Examiner had a word about him and his ilk. In a cartoon a menacing-looking darkie shouts: "Don't be bumping into me, white man. I'se tough, Remembah the Civil War is over I'se tough."

Between World Wars I and II, a few liberals and radicals hoped that the press and the public would knock off the crude stuff and start down the path of racial enlightenment. Black editors knew better. They were still fighting tough battles to get the white press to stop stereotyping black men. Whenever a crime was committed, if a black was involved or suspected, newspapers almost always mentioned it. In case some were slow to make the connection, they would plaster a black face across the page.

NOTE: Black folks, as always, tried to find some humor in the situation. They joked that if a black ever wanted to get the white press to write about them, commit a crime and make sure the victim was white..

The defeat of Hitler and America's ascension to superpowerdom ushered in the American Century. This was supposed to be the era that American military might and economic muscle would bring permanent prosperity and freedom to the world. It would be an era when the winds of racial change would end segregation and race hate forever.

For a short while it seemed that blacks might get a little breathing space. The civil rights movement pricked the consciences of many whites. Congress, the White House and the Courts, with varying degrees of enthusiasm, finally relented and eliminated legal segregation. But, with the death of Martin Luther King, Jr. and Malcolm X, the collapse of the civil rights movement, political repression and the self-destruction of black power radicalism, young blacks were organizationally adrift.

Recession and economic shrinkage began to wreak havoc on the black poor. Many whites once again began to use terms about black men that sounded faintly reminiscent of the by-gone days, "law and order," "welfare cheats," "crime in the streets," "subculture of violence," "subculture of poverty," "culturally deprived" and "lack of family values."

By the end of the Reagan years, the language got rougher. The press now routinely tossed around terms like "crime prone," "war zone," "gang infested," "crack plagued," "drug turfs," "drug zombies," "violence scarred," "ghetto outcasts" and "ghetto poverty syndrome." Some, in the press, let it all hang out and called black criminals "scum," "leeches" and "losers." Their pictures routinely began to appear on the front pages, and for some strange reason they were all mostly black males.

NOTE: Why drag up what happened a century ago? Americans don't believe any of this anymore. On October 31, 1993, two students at Yosemite High School in Oakhurst, a community just south of San Francisco, showed up at the school's Halloween party in Ku Klux Klan costumes. A third student wore black face.

The two students proceeded to stage a mock lynching of the "black." The three self-appointed white Knights may not have known any better. But what about school officials, parents and the other students? The three won prizes for their costumes. Students said it was "cool, like original." The principal took no disciplinary action against them. That's why!

2

The Fine Art of Black Male Bashing

I didn't think Chuck Stuart would do it. By committing suicide, Chuck confounded the media and blew the lid off what *Newsweek* called the "great hoax." The joke was on a whole lot of black men in Boston. None of whom were laughing.

On a dreary October night in 1989, the bloody bodies of Stuart and his pregnant wife, Carol were found in the front seat of their car. It was parked in a dark alley next to the predominantly black projects in Boston's Mission Hill section. Carol Stuart was dead, and so was her baby. Chuck suffering from a massive gunshot wound to his stomach was rushed to the hospital. On the way, a police officer who accompanied him asked him, "You see who shot you." Chuck miraculously possessed enough of his faculties to answer, "a black male."

At the hospital, Chuck kept repeating the words like a broken record, "Shot me, shot my wife, black male." The nurses and attendants thought it was a little peculiar that a man fighting for his life could say so clearly that his attacker was "a black male." These were mere trifles that Boston newspapers weren't concerned with at the time. The crime was simply too ghastly. A white, middle-class, professional woman was dead and her husband was severely wounded. They were the "Camelot couple" and Chuck had uttered the three terrifying words, "a black male." The apocalyptic nightmare of black crime had finely shattered the nervous peace in white suburbia.

The stampede was on. The killing, said one editor, had "sparked particular outrage." The *Boston Globe* and *Boston Herald* filled their pages with horrific stories about desperate, violence-prone, young, black men terrorizing the city. Men such as these were capable of anything and the Stuart murder proved it. The *Herald* publisher seemed positively giddy at the public response "we couldn't print papers fast enough to keep up with the demand."

The politicians weren't far behind. They whiffed a big story and jumped in with both feet. The mayor, city council members and state legislators thundered against the lawlessness, offered big rewards for the killer(s), and promised to hunt them down. The Republican State Committee wasn't satisfied. It demanded that the legislature immediately reinstitute the death penalty. Republican state legislators had their marching orders and swore that they wouldn't rest until the legislature reinstated it.

Meanwhile, black Bostonians knew that there would be hell to pay. They braced themselves for the furious onslaught. It came fast. For days, dozens of police roamed the streets of Mission Hill and the surrounding black areas looking for suspects. The horror stories began almost immediately. Young black men told scary tales of police making them crawl, kneel and lay belly down on the ground while they ran makes on them. Others told how police made them pull their pants down in public streets while they searched them. Dozens were hauled away for questioning. Others were arrested on a variety of charges. Some claimed that they were beaten.

Eventually they latched on to thirty-nine year old Willie Bennett. He was the perfect patsy, an ex-convict with a long rap sheet. It probably would have worked, except for a few doubters who didn't just read the newspapers, they also read Chuck Stuart. They were suspicious of his actions and his motives. A relative who knew that Chuck was really the triggerman had also begun to talk. The noose began to tighten around him. But Chuck cheated the hangman by jumping into Boston Bay.

Case closed? Suppose the doubters hadn't raised questions? Suppose a relative had kept his mouth shut? Suppose Chuck hadn't committed suicide? Suppose, suppose, suppose. Take them away and Bennett almost certainly would have been tried and convicted for the murder. If there had been a death penalty, he would have gotten it.

Was the press irresponsible in fanning the flames of hysteria and racial paranoia? The editors were in no mood to offer *mea culpas*. They were defiant and unrepentant. "Hey," they squealed, "we were just doing our job and reporting the news." "Look," they protested, "the public wanted information." "Listen," they shouted, "black men do commit a lot of crimes." In its wrap up story on the case, *Newsweek* took a big swing at black leaders who groused about "negative press reporting on the black community." It accused them of "trying to have it both ways."

The point sailed way over the heads of the magazine's editors. The issue is not the coverage, it's the type of coverage. No one is telling the press not to cover crime stories about blacks, but cover other stories, too. When the press obsessively focuses on criminal acts by some blacks and excludes everything else, look what happens. Boston newspapers played the crime beat hard, and predictably got the Pavlovan response. Politicians talked tough about law and order and scored more brownie points with white voters. The police took license to violate basic rights in the black neighborhoods. And white suburbanites were scared stiff.

Newsweek did ask one correct question. If Carol Stuart had been a black woman would the press have cared? I also ask, if Chuck had said that the murderer was a white man would the press have run the scare stories it did run? Let's find the answer. Remember the media images of black men a century ago? Today, when editors lace their features on African-Americans with terms such as "crime prone," "crack heads," "educational cripples," "poverty ravaged" and "gang ridden," what's really changed?

Despite what *Newsweek* says, the media craze with ghetto crime, drugs, gangs and poverty titillates and scares whites (including many blacks and other people of color too). It absolves the press of the responsibility to report, probe and find answers as to why black men do all the allegedly "brutal" things they do.

NOTE: It was a good thing for George Bush in 1988 that much of the media didn't probe too deeply into the real causes of crime. If they had, Republican strategists could not have played the black brute image like a finely tuned Stradivarius violin. They cast escaped Massachusetts convict Willie Horton in the brute role and used him to batter Democratic presidential candidate Michael Dukakis as "soft on crime." The big lead Dukakis had over Bush evaporated faster than a disappearing act by Houdini.

The media can't feign ignorance that they distort the news. A multi-part story in the *Los Angeles Times* in December 1990, proved convincingly that editors knew that race bias was buried deep in news and features.

How could it be any other way? The men and women who run the show in the media are hardly neutral or objective bystanders who just report the news. Their tastes, preferences, personal beliefs, values, outlook, class, money, status and, of course, prejudices bear directly on what they consider news, and how they cover it.

II

It's been that way for years. The men who trailblazed, molded and shaped the news business were petty potentates. They answered to no man, country, flag or even God. They had power and they exercised it with reckless abandon. In the press room, their word was law. Once *Los Angeles Times* publisher Norman Chandler bluntly asked his managing editor, "Do we have to run this? Do we have to put this in?" It was phrased as a question, but the editor knew better. It was a command.

Time-Life founder, Henry Luce cut right to the chase shouting. "I don't believe in objective journalism." They wanted men around them with whom they felt comfortable playing tennis, golf or smoozing at lunch. Men with whom they didn't have to watch their language. If someone blurted out a racist or sexist wisecrack, the fellows laughed and nobody was offended because they all spoke the same language.

Washington Post owner, Phil Graham, golfed regularly with *New York Times* ace James Reston. *Times* heir, Iphigene Sulzberger told her publisher husband Arthur (remember she was a woman and in those days public decisions were made by the men) to surround himself with only "fine young men, intelligent and proper," who would make decisions at the paper.

The pioneers are long gone but their ghosts still rattle around the editorial board rooms. More than ninety-eight percent of those "proper" men making the decisions about what's news are still white.

This isn't to say that "proper" blacks wouldn't necessarily make the same decisions about content and coverage. If they share the same upper crust mindset, values and background, like to hang out at the same country clubs and on the tennis courts and believe that their poorer black brethren are crime prone and derelict, the news would still look the same. In an age when the media can turn Hollywood madam Heidi into an instant superstar, when even the barest scintilla of scandal and kinkiness can send news editors salivating, and where corporate control is in the tight hands of privileged white conservative males, stories on black achievement will still take a backseat (if that) to a juicy ghetto murder or rape story any day.

III

But maybe I'm wrong. It's been several years since *Newsweek* gingerly chided the press for its panic reporting on the Stuart case. Has anything changed? To find out, I made an informal survey of the big five, *Time Magazine, Newsweek, Los Angeles Times, Wall Street Journal* and the *New York Times* for the month of August 1993.

NOTE: It is true that the general public gets its news from TV. But TV still gets its news/story ideas from the major dailies.

To keep it simple, I excluded the three major 1993 domestic stories, the Reginald Denny beating trial in Los Angeles, the Thirtieth anniversary of the March on Washington and the Rodney King case from the survey. I focused on just the "routine" daily coverage. They were: crime (I stopped count-ing at 21), welfare-poverty-homelessness (5), black achieve-ment (0). Here's what the press did and didn't say.

Los Angeles Times, August 23, 1993, p. 1

In a multi-part story on "youth in trouble," the *Times* profiled the cases of several (black) teens. Seventeen year old Gregory is one. Gregory has been in and out of detention for drug selling, vandalism and truancy. The story line is that Gregory is not really a bad kid but was led astray by an "unpredictable father." He's a violent man, who killed his wife, bought drugs from his son and eventually deserted him. The *Times* makes only scant mention of the fact that the father was also a mentally disturbed, physically disabled Vietnam veteran.

The story did not say whether he received financial assistance, veteran's benefits; and, importantly hospital-ization, therapy and quality medical care to overcome the trauma and shock of his Vietnam experience. Many of these men were discarded, forgotten or maligned by the general public as dope smoking misfits.

A study by the Commission on Quality Care for the mentally disabled in New York found that thousands who suffered chronic emotional disorders did not receive quality in-home care and were dumped on the streets with no means of support. This might have shed some light on why Gregory's father ended up the way he did. But, that was another issue. In the editor's eyes the better story was about a crime addicted, black teen spawned by a derelict, convict black father.

New York Times, August 31, 1993, p. 1

Since the report by Daniel Patrick Moynihan on the black

family in 1965, we have been constantly reminded that absentee black men have turned black families into a "tangle of pathology." Bill Clinton, George Bush and Dan Quayle made the family a big issue during the 1992 presidential campaign. Conservatives use it as a battering ram against the evils of welfarism and big government. *Newsweek* in a cover story feature dredged up the issue and blamed the sorry plight of the ghetto on "A World Without Fathers." Anyone can make a compelling case for black male deviance and family destabilization. Here's how. Jumble income and population figures, downplay the achievements of the black middle class, ignore the profound gender role changes in American society; then pretend that the Reagan-Bush cuts in job, education, and family support programs benefited the poor.

But what happens when an article does try to put a positive spin on single dads who raise their kids? Howard, Fred and Troy are trying to do that. Howard and Fred are white. Troy is black. Howard is described as a successful businessman who can afford a maid to help raise his three sons. Fred a former army sergeant, is a UPS driver, happily raising his young daughter. Both men come off as solid middle-class guys, sans wives.

Troy, on the other hand, makes his living on a $16,000 year income as a data processing clerk. He says he "didn't remember his father," and "he grew up in a rough-edged neighborhood." Fred and Howard, from the impression conveyed by the article, were naturally experienced fathers. Troy was different. He was "determined to be a good father but unsure how to gain the skills."

Did the *Times* ever wonder that perhaps Troy's uncertainty about parenting was due less to his lack of "natural" skills and more to his marginal job and low income? Howard and Fred were older men with income, business and professional status. This made the crucial difference in their parenting success. The *New York Times* may not know it, but there are other black men in "rough-edged neighborhoods" who are "experienced fathers." Better still, there are even some black men who don't live in "rough-edged neighborhoods" that are experienced fathers, too.

Time Magazine, August 16, 1993, p. 45

Time certainly did not have men like Troy in mind in its feature on carjacking. But the pictures of the arrested young men looked suspiciously like him. They were all young black males. The writer brought the usual customary editorial flourishes, the "thugs opened fire," "rolling danger" and it "fuels a kind of hysteria." The writer reminded readers that "young men in the inner city are the most likely victims of violent crimes."

The problem with all this is that it had little to do with the story or the crime. In a side bar feature, *Time* admitted that half the thefts are orchestrated by organized car theft rings. They sell the parts to chop shops, (salvage yards that pay up to $5,000 for the hot goods). Some insurance companies have even gotten in on the organized thievery. They will buy parts marked-up two to three times their store value.

The larceny takes place far from the borders of the ghettos. Two white professional thieves who made good livings swiping autos in Philadelphia were profiled. One was a veteran and a "good" family man. He almost bragged about his "profession." Although he was arrested nine times, he never served any prison time. In the article, the pair came off as regular, although slightly crooked Joes.

Who said there is no honor among thieves?

Wall Street Journal, August 18, 1993, p. 1

Now let's look at Glen Hutchins. He's a thirtyish businessman with an MBA and law degree from Harvard. He
wears $1,000 pin stripe suits and sports the well coifed look
of the 1990s. He makes decisions "swiftly under pressure."
He helps charities. He is a kind, considerate and caring
family man. But there's a shadow over Glen's work. He is a
member of the Thomas Lee firm in Boston. He specializes in
leveraged buyouts of near bankrupt companies (the *Journal*
calls them "losers") and "realigning" them. Anchor Advanced Products in Morristown, Tennessee was one of those
companies Glen "realigned."

The realignment cost dozens of jobs and afflicted
economic misery on the town. Nothing personal, just
business. This is all perfectly legal of course, but I thought I'd
throw it in just to show that when young white middle-class
males wheel and deal, no editor or writer calls them "derelict,"
"irresponsible" or heaven forbid, "criminal." After all, in
this world there have to be "losers."

Newsweek, August 21, 1993, p. 40

Even when the press tries to be "objective," scratch the
surface a little, peer underneath and the bias lurks. This
Newsweek cover story "Wild in the Streets," reports that teen
violence is not just a problem of the ghetto. White
suburbanites fear that they can be mugged or murdered too,
not by marauding blacks, but by the kid next door (or in their
own house).

The article ticks off a spate of gruesome shootings,
beatings and stabbings that have shocked suburbia. In
Houston, it was a rape strangulation. In Dartmouth, Massa-

chusetts, it was a classroom murder. In Ft. Lauderdale, Florida it was a beating and stabbing. The culprits were white teens. *Newsweek* was the paragon of objectivity. It skipped the gore, guts and hysteria. It made no judgments. There was no sneaky editorializing, no clinical analysis of the killer's personality. Just the facts.

When the accounts of violence shifted from the suburbs to the inner city "war zone," *Newsweek* loaded up. Suddenly, we were in no-man's land. It was "gang riddled South Central Los Angeles" with its "blood splattered sidewalks" and where kids "grow up to the sounds of sirens and gunshots." They live in "neighborhoods where trauma seems normal" and the "normal rules of behavior don't apply."

There's danger at every turn in this black no-man's land where wild people roam. Six year old Shaakara tells us about that. He lives in the no-man's land of Chicago's teeming ghetto. Shaakara describes in graphic detail how a man slashed a baby and then beat to death its grandmother. In Detroit, a nineteen year old tells how three of his homies, Bootsie, Shadow and Showtime were killed. "I saw the blood from the back of his head spread on the snow."

No one should minimize the pain and shock of seeing friends and relatives murdered whether in the ghetto or suburb. But, accounts like this do just that. Are we to believe that no blood spread on the ground from the kid who was bashed in the head and dumped in a quarry by six white teens in Ft. Lauderdale? *Newsweek* never tells us. Maybe that's because there names weren't Bootsie, Shadow and Showtime and they didn't live among people where the "normal rules of behavior don't apply."

Los Angeles Times, August 16, 1993, p. B1

Michael Yocum, thirty-eight, is one of an estimated

40,000 to 75,000 people in Los Angeles County who on any given night prowl the streets searching for food and shelter. Even though many of these men are white, Yocum isn't. He's black. As such, he's guaranteed a featured spot in a story on the homeless.

Yocum is pictured sitting at a window with the lonely, forlorn look of a desperate man. He subsists on welfare and whatever he can get scavenging. We're told that he can't work because he has a bad back. Even if Yocum's back was in tip top condition, it might not change his plight. During the Reagan-Bush years, the unemployment rate for black men was double to triple that of white men, their earnings dropped to seventy-four percent of white males.

More than one-third of the jobs lost during the 1990-1991 economic downturn were lost by blacks. Asians, Latinos and white males all gained jobs. A Black male college graduate was more than two- and one-half times more likely to be unemployed than a white college graduate. Men like Yocum watched while industry packed up and fled the inner city to the suburbs taking thousands of jobs. If Yocum lucked up and got one of these jobs, he'd go into deep debt trying to pay the steep transportation costs getting there.

Even so, in countless interviews, men like Yocum tell sad tales of layoffs and firings after plant closings, followed by dead end searches for non-existent jobs. Occasionally, one of these men will turn the tables on a skeptical reporter and ask if the reporter thinks he gets perverse enjoyment sleeping under tunnels, underpasses and bus stops in the heat, cold and rain? Does the reporter think its fun being preyed on by thieves and harassed by the police?

Maybe that's why one brother I saw begging near a busy intersection in the posh Marina del Rey section of Los Angeles carried a sign that read, "I'm not a bum, addict, psycho, lazy or stupid. I want to work." He knew exactly what many whites thought about him, and he answered back.

Wall Street Journal, August 31, 1993, p. 10

The editorial writer for the *Journal* didn't drive by that corner and see the poor fellow's sign. On the occasion of the Thirtieth anniversary of the March on Washington, the *Journal* lectured NAACP executive director Ben Chavis and Urban League director John Jacobs on their "responsibility" as black leaders.

Chavis and Jacobs had raised the *Journal's* neo-conservative hackles by demanding that Washington foot the bill for a fifty billion dollar Marshall style domestic bail-out plan for the inner cities. The *Journal* grumbled that these "leaders" should stop looking to Sugar Daddy Washington for help. It assured readers that other than a few pockets of bigotry "buried in the psyches of some Americans," racism was dead. Black folks should quit blaming whites for ghetto misery, forget about government programs and stop haranguing corporations about affirmative action. Chavis and Jacobs would be wiser to tell their people to develop:
a) "respect for the rule of law;"
b) "renewed reverence for hard work;"
c) "individual responsibility;" and,
d) "stable families."

Lazy, criminal, derelict and immoral (sex crazed); did the *Journal* miss anything? This would have warmed the hearts of the white gentlemen-scholars of the Nineteenth Century who used pretty much the same arguments to explain black inferiority.

It's a cliché, but it bears repeating when it comes to media reporting on black males. The more things change the more they stay the same. It's a pity. The men and women who write these articles aren't inherently evil or malicious. Some consider themselves good liberals, sensitive to social causes and issues. Some are even charter members of the NAACP, the National Urban League, and give to the United Negro College Fund. Some agree that they should hire more blacks (if they're qualified, of course). Some have black friends and acquaintances. They don't deliberately slam black men. They don't have to.

Over time, the ancient racial stereotypes have been confirmed, validated and deepened until they have taken on a life of their own. If editors constantly feature young black males as gang members or drug dealers and not Merit Achievement Scholars or National Science Foundation scholarship winners because they don't believe they exist or that young black males are capable of achieving those distinctions, then the news becomes a grim self-fulfilling prophecy.

Whether racial stereotypes predominate because of benign neglect or savage intent is irrelevant, the end result is the same. Many whites (and some blacks) shiver in terror around young black males. This gives conservatives more ammunition to decapitate job, education and social programs; to torpedo affirmative action gains, stymie civil rights legislation and obliterate civil liberties. It's all done under the pretense of the big black scare.

Willie Bennett knows all about this. While sitting in a cell at the Norfolk County jail, he was told of Chuck's suicide. This exonerated him. He should have been happy, but he wasn't. He said simply, "My life and my family's life have been ruined and no one is willing to take responsibility." Unfortunately, *Newsweek* and the nation's press had no answer for him nor the thousands of other Willie Bennetts victimized by the fine art of black male bashing.

3

From Slavery to the Sports Arena

I really miss Jimmy "The Greek" Snyder. I miss him so much I almost wrote to CBS executives asking them to rehire him. I felt the only reason they fired him as a sports commentator in 1988 was because he was honest. The Greek said that blacks dominate major sport because they were "bred to be that way by the slave owner." He only said what many of the white folks who make the decisions in the sports profession really think about black athletes.

NOTE: CBS received more than 2,000 letters after "The Greek" was fired. In the beginning the fans supported CBS. But HMMMMMM, after they thought about his words a little more sentiment swung sharply against CBS. Many thought, maybe the old Greek was right. In the words of one fan "the truth always hurts."

Anyway, "The Greek" has a better memory than most. During the plantation days, when the white masters got tired of counting their cotton dollars and playing bedroom footsie with the cullud house servants, they would round up their pals and arrange a little sport. They would select two of their biggest, brawniest and blackest bucks, and toss them into a make shift ring. The masters would guzzle gallons of whiskey and rum, crack jokes and make big wagers, while the two bucks banged each other to a bloody pulp.

Before he escaped from slavery, black abolitionist Frederick Douglass watched it all with disgust, "only those wild and low sports peculiar to semicivilized people were encouraged." For their bumps and bruises, the black bucks might get a little better food, an extra set of hand me downs and, if especially lucky, their freedom. These black bucks were master's prized gladiators. They had to be treated a little special.

The end of slavery brought a halt to master's sporting life with his prized bucks. As free men, their services were no longer needed. Even in the formative years of major league baseball, there was just too much money and prestige involved to let them play. For years to come, the only thing black in baseball were the player's shoes. Black athletes could showcase their talents in the Negro Leagues barnstorming through backwater towns and playing in pastures, cow fields or ramshackle lots.

In the early years of basketball, they could join the Globetrotters and play clowns, buffoons and "Uncle Toms." A few found some glory (but no money) in football and track only because in those days they were considered bush league sports. As long as they kept away from white women, they were tolerated in boxing since it was considered a sport for brutes anyway. When Jack Johnson forgot that, the sport (and the country) KO'd him fast.

Black men, however, were just too good at running, jumping and whacking those balls. It was only a matter of time before the new masters in sport would remember those bucks again. Jackie Robinson broke the color bar in baseball; Chuck Cooper in basketball. After that the rush was on to get as many of them as white folks could stomach at one time. Some fans grumbled. Some owners resisted. Some white players talked of boycotts. It was like trying to stop the tide with sandcastles. Black players were in major sports to stay.

The racial complexion of sports had changed but the mentality of many of those who ran it, promoted it and broadcast it didn't. They were still black bucks, employed for the amusement and entertainment of white folks. When an occasional critic like sports sociologist Harry Edwards complained that blacks were still underpaid, underappreciated and unaccepted as social equals, sports writers and executives quickly reminded him that slaves don't make millions of dollars, receive college educations and live in palatial estates in the suburbs.

Edwards should shut up and be grateful. If it wasn't for sports, these guys would be selling hot clothes in Harlem, peddling dope in Watts or carjacking on Chicago's West side. Eventually, they'd all wind up serving hard time in some joint. Edwards reminded them that some of them ended up doing that anyway once they were dumped from a team because of injury, a run-in with a coach or fell from grace with an owner.

Edwards further reminded them that even successful black athletes were often discarded like a dirty jock strap once their glory days were over. They did not step from the court, grid iron or the cinders into Congress or the Senate like Jack Kemp, Bob Mathias and Bill Bradley. Yeah, there was ex-Olympian Ralph Metcalf who went to Congress, but that was another time and place, and how often did anyone ever mention him as a possible presidential candidate?

The way Edwards could tell what many sportsmen

really thought of black athletes was the way they were educated. How many were majoring in law, medicine or engineering? Instead, how many were majoring in physical education, sports therapy, social studies or simply "undeclared." Their graduation rate from colleges was a national disgrace.

When Edwards cracked that a high school athlete had a better chance of being hit on the head by a meteor then making a pro team he was not being tart. He was only suggesting that maybe it was time for those aspiring Jordans and Emmit Smiths in the ghetto (and their parents too) to re-examine their priorities. There was nothing wrong with young black men spending as much time preparing for English and algebra exams as they did practicing hand-offs and power spin moves around the hoop, even if it did make some coaches mad. If they had any doubts, they should take a closer look at the fate of many of their million dollar, All-American, black heroes.

II

Ask for more money. When former Los Angeles Ram running back, Eric Dickerson did, many sports writers carried on a relentless vendetta against him. They called him a whiner, overrated, overpaid and an ingrate. They recycled old articles telling the public that pro athletes are really just grown men playing kid's sports. They're not like Joe Blue Collar who has to sweat and scuffle for his $497.59 weekly take home pay.

Dickerson could have answered, "true, but he'll make that for the next forty years with no risk of blown knees, broken arms, legs or necks. He could have said that no one squawks when they pay Frank Sinatra or Bob Hope long dough for appearances even though their best days are way behind them. If he did say that, it wouldn't mean much. When the sports writers got through with him, the poor guy felt like he should have paid the owners for the privilege of playing.

Get injured. Los Angeles Dodger, Darryl Strawberry and the Houston Rockets, Hakeem Olajuwon know about this one. Many sportswriters called them malingerers and shirkers. They accused them of being con artists out to stick the team up for more dollars. Black men aren't like normal people (white people). With all that muscle and brawn, black men are supposed to be impervious to injury and pain. Even if they come armed with a dozen letters from doctors and specialists supporting their injury claim, it won't stop the owners and sportswriters from putting out the word that they're "injury prone."

This is a polite way of saying they're damaged goods. If the black athlete is smart he'll make no big ticket item expenses, save his money and plan on a speedy retirement because his days are numbered. Black damaged goods aren't kept on injured reserve or taxi squads very long. And they damn sure can't be long-term bench warmers. Those are the quota spots reserved for marginal white players.

Be your own man. How many sportswriters still hummed "I like Mike" when they found out Jordan had something more important to do than grin at President Bush at the White House after the Bulls won their first world championship. How many gushed oohs and aahs for Air Jordan when he demanded the right to spend his money anyway he wanted. If that meant gambling on golf, black jack or pinochle it was nobody's business but his own. These were the same guys who chuckled and winked at the off the field drinking and carousing antics of former Oakland Raider quarterback Ken "snake" Stabler. There were no indignant articles that accused him of "damaging the sport." Naw, he was just a good ole boy having fun YEEEEHAHHH.

When Mike mildly complained that the sportswriters were being "unfair," they huffed that they had indulged him for years, practically made his rep for him. And they allowed him to make millions. Gee! I always thought that the crowds mobbed the arenas, and the sportswriters greedily snapped up their complimentary press box seats to see the most exciting and entertaining athlete in sports.

NOTE: This item was buried on the second to the last page in the Saturday, October 9, 1993, sports section in the Los Angeles Times. After an investigation of Mike's gambling activities, NBA Commissioner David Stern announced there was "absolutely no evidence that Jordan violated league rules." I guess the sports writers must have missed this, since few of them mentioned it in their columns. If Stern had found some evidence that he had....need I finish?

<u>Be outspoken</u>. Football's Jim Brown, baseball's Reggie Jackson and basketball's Bill Russell were proud black men who had more on their minds then just Xs and Os, RBIs and rebounds. They also had opinions about race, politics and how their people were treated in America. This was a bad mistake. The press branded them "black militants." Yes, they got their money and fame. It was hard not to begrudge them that since they were the best athletes in their sport. But, the sports writers laced their columns with innuendoes that the sport might be better off if they shut up and played ball.

III

Even when black athletes act like deaf mutes on social

issues, don't raise a stink about salaries, behave like choir-boys and have cast iron constitutions, chances are that sportswriters will still use racial double speak when they talk about them and white players.

I take my cue from Monday Night football. I've watched nearly every game starting with the first game between the New York Jets and the Cleveland Browns in September 1970. Over the years, I compiled these code words from the sports chatter of the announcers:

White Player: Heady.
Black Player: A burner, a speedster, or can motor.
WP: Good work habits.
BP: Moody, a head case.
WP: Cagey, disciplined.
BP: Erratic.
WP: A project (This means that the team's owner is willing to spend time and money waiting for him to produce.).
BP: Raw talent, but doesn't live up to his potential.
WP: Fearless, courageous.
BP: Hears footsteps.
WP: Aggressive, a hustler.
BP: A real animal.

Occasionally, an announcer got excited and forgot to use racial double speak. This happened to Howard Cosell in 1983. He called the Washington Redskins wide receiver, Alvin Garett "a little monkey." Cosell promptly got called out on it. If he had simply called him a "burner," "aggressive" or even a "scooter," he'd have been home free. So bring "The Greek" back. He made the game so much simpler. He never kept the brothers guessing about where they stood. That's why Jackie Robinson said in his autobiography, "I never had it made."

4

Doing the **W**rong **T**hing by **S**pike

I think Spike knows that they hate him. The *They* are the film critics, studio executives, black conservatives, black militants and black feminists. In recent years, they've all ganged up on the brother for his alleged sins.

With many studio executives and film critics, it was pure hate and envy from day one. They called him arrogant, abrasive and a jerk. They really didn't like him because he's an uppity nigger that speaks his mind and happens to be damn good at what he does.

Yes, I know that they bankrolled and promoted his films. Some critics even claimed that if it wasn't for Hollywood, Spike would be shining shoes in front of a subway station in Brooklyn. Wrong! Hollywood didn't make him. It made money off of him.

His first film, *She's Gotta Have It*, was a no-budget film made with lots of credit cards and much arm twisting of friends and relatives to help out. *School Daze* was a low budget, mom and pop shoe string job, too. When the films raked in the cash, the studio executives took notice. They loosened the purse strings, but not much.

Jungle Fever and *Do the Right Thing* became huge hits. Compared to the legion of other stinkers that Hollywood releases and routinely writes off when they bomb, these two films were still nestled deep in Hollywood's low rent district. They were controversial, however, and there's nothing better than controversy to get Hollywood panting, tongues wagging and cash registers jingling.

Then Spike and Hollywood found Malcolm X. Why not? After five years, Malcolm had been glorified by rappers, hyped by the street side T-shirt and cap hawkers, seized by the fashion industry, packaged and sanitized by Madison Avenue and defanged politically by politicians like Dan Quayle and celebrities like Madonna. Studio executives hoped that *Malcolm X*, the film, might even bag some of the cross-over crowd. Many hip hop whites, Latinos and Asians were also wearing X hats and T-shirts. Someone even spotted Bill Clinton sporting an X cap.

Warner Bros. upped the cash. But, it was still wary. That's when the conflict began. They complained that Spike was spending too much money and taking too much time with "the project." The film critics eagerly saw it as a chance to take more cheap shots at him. They called him a cry baby, complainer and a spoiled brat. The few extra million dollars Spike was asking to finish the film was bare pocket change to the studios. *Far and Away* cost $60 million. *Honey I Blew Up the Kids*, $40 million; *Patriot Games*, $65 million; and *Batman*, $55 million. The studios didn't bat an eye at these costs.

They happily shelled out $12 million to Arnie for his role in *Terminator II*, and $8 million to Tom, pretty blue eyes, Cruse for his part in *Far and Away*. Their salaries could have practically bankrolled Spike's film.

Warner Bros., embarrassed, finally piped down, and ponied up the rest of the bread when Lee got his pals Oprah, Air Jordan, Magic and Bill Cosby to kick in some spare change. The film critics merely bided their time. When the film was released they got their revenge. They called it a flop before the projectors were barely warm. Columnist Coleman McCarthy, a self-proclaimed liberal, found nothing redeeming about Malcolm's life, the film, and though he didn't say it directly, the filmmaker.

This is the same bunch who turned into deaf mutes after the eternal revivals of *Gone With the Wind* and *Birth of a Nation*, or gushed over them as "classics." *Gone With the Wind* seared into the memories of generations of school children, the myth of the happy-go-lucky, faithful darky. *Birth of a Nation* glorified the Ku Klux Klan. And, who said the South lost the Civil War. Zippity Doo Dah!

II

Anyway, Spike could handle them. He never had any illusion that they would ever accept an arrogant, skinny-assed, black man in their circle.

Black folks were another matter. The black conservatives complained that Spike was whipping up race hatred and inciting violence in his films. As a guest, I had to sit through nearly an hour on one radio talk show listening to one of them denounce Spike for showing the tape of the Rodney King beating and burning the American flag in the opening scene. The scene took about a minute or so. I wondered what this erstwhile critic did to amuse himself during the rest of the film's three hours and twenty minutes?

Black militants, instead of backing him, back-bit him. They yelped that he would defile Malcolm's sacred image by turning him into a dope dealing, second-story thief, desperate to get under a white woman's skirt. They weren't buying Spike's sensible explanation that he was not making an underground documentary for arty farty revival houses, but a real commercial movie, for real theaters and real moviegoers.

They didn't listen when Spike said that the film would erase the image of Malcolm as a hate filled fanatic who called whites "devils" and introduced thousands of people (including many young blacks) to Malcolm's life and ideology. They forgot that one of the qualities that made Malcolm great was his ability to admit his mistakes and re-evaluate his ideas. He was able to look deep into the scarred abyss of his soul and America's soul and wage intense struggle to change both.

Some black feminists ragged on Spike *and* Malcolm. They claimed that Malcolm was really a sexist and that the Nation of Islam treated women like kitchen help. They didn't think Spike portrayed women much better in his films. *She's Gotta Have It* supposedly proved that. They twisted it around to make Nola, the lead character, a sexually exploited Barbie doll for her men. She wasn't. When one of her lovers pesters her to tell him if he's as good as her other two lovers, she says "that's the dumbest thing you've said." He pleads some more, "but I love you." She knows better, "You're not in love with me. You're in love with my lovemaking. Don't mess it up." This doesn't sound to me like a woman who's a ding bat plaything of the fellows.

III

Then there's Malcolm. To call him a male chauvinist is like asking a cave man to master an advanced MAC Quadra computer system in one sitting. Malcolm was a product of his times and thinking. Feminism for black men and women during Malcolm's life was not even a word then, let alone a full movement or ideology. Forget what Malcolm said, how did he treat Betty Shabazz and his children? Betty had no complaints. She said Malcolm was a kind, considerate, loving parent and husband. Malcolm did not treat her nor regard her as an inferior. Spike took pains to show that Betty was a strong, independent woman. Malcolm respected and appreciated her.

NOTE: *The women in the Nation of Islam didn't think it was a badge of inferiority when the brothers called them "sister" instead of "bitch," and did not abuse or beat them but made them feel honored. My guess is there are a lot of black women who would like the same thing today.*

After his break with the Nation, Malcolm rethought many of his ideas about the role of black women in the movement. Three months before his murder he said, "I am proud of the role that women, our women, have played in the freedom struggle and I am in favor of them having full freedom because they have made a greater contribution than many of our men."

IV

That's not all that bothers me about Spike's black critics. They are the same folks that were stone silent or drooled over films like *Boyz N the Hood.* They proclaimed the young black filmmakers geniuses for capturing the gritty reality of the ghetto. Geniuses? Take a closer look. They glorified guns, cash and dope. They reduced the English vocabulary to a vile stream of "Goddamns" and "motherfuckers." They savaged black women as "bitches" and "hos"and each other as "niggers" and "bitches."

Was it an accident that the same Hollywood film critics who made a growth industry out of mugging Spike went ga ga over these films? Why did they think it was so great to show young blacks cursing, fighting and killing each other? Or maybe they were just happy that the filmmakers didn't blame whites for the crisis of the ghetto.

That was Spike's problem. He played it to close to the vest. He thought that black folks occasionally might want to see themselves as something other than crooks, clowns and charity cases on the screen. He believed that he could sneak films with positive messages through the Hollywood cracks. But, Spike's a resilient guy. He'll keep doing the right thing in his films, even when others don't do the right thing by him.

5

Thomas, Tyson and Tall Tales

I never believed Anita Hill. Not because I thought that she deliberately lied about Deh Judge, Clarence Thomas. Nor because the issue of sex harassment is trivial.

I didn't believe her because she raised the issue at the wrong time, in the wrong place and with the wrong people. I didn't believe her because to this day, she and many feminists are still using Deh Judge as a club to bludgeon the nation on the issue of sex harassment.

NOTE: Sex discrimination is illegal. Yet despite a Supreme Court ruling that proclaims sexual "intimidation, ridicule and insult" illegal, when and what constitutes sex harassment is still subject to wildly varying interpretations by individuals, courts and state laws.

The newspaper polls consistently showed that the majority of blacks didn't believe her either. That included many black women. The way some of the black women I know reacted told me why they didn't believe her. The day Anita testified, they were livid. Two were so angry they cried. These are not stupid, naive women. They were not mad at Anita because she broke the "code of silence" within the black community on sex abuse. They did not agree with Deh Judge's personal or political conservatism. They didn't really give a damn whether he was confirmed or not.

They were mad at Anita because they believed that black men and women should work and struggle together. They were mad at Anita because they believed she was being used by whites to get at a brother. Their anger tells much about how the black working class perceives feminism, gender issues and racism. Issues that civil rights leaders, feminists and many black radicals deftly dance around. I'll come back to this.

II

Deh Judge. When Anita said he talked about "Long Dong Silver," pubic hairs on coke bottles and made nasty gestures, Deh Judge didn't need his law degree from Yale to know he was in deep shit. Sexual perversion and black men instantly rattle ugly tremors in the hidden recesses of the collective psyche of many whites. Deh Judge sweated. For an instant, he saw all the painstaking years he spent grinning, buck dancing, shuffling and playing the good nigger flushed down the stool. He could make Heritage Foundation speeches until the cows came home. He could shout all the content of character, not color of skin drivel he wanted. It couldn't flush his reputation back up.

Deh Judge didn't have to think about his response. He screamed that this was a "high tech lynching of an uppity black man." If white Americans and the senators believed

Anita, and many secretly did, including the ones who claimed they didn't, Deh Judge would have been run out of Washington on a rail. But, when you're black and conservative, politics makes strange bedfellows. If Anita had been white even that wouldn't have saved him. Instead of being confirmed as a sitting judge, Deh Judge might have been sitting in front of a judge.

Feminists loudly complained that the Senators gorillad Anita. If Deh Judge had been a white man, they wouldn't have had to worry. Nobody would have believed her anyway. Hill-Thomas would have been parlor gossip quietly buried behind closed doors.

If Anita was rough housed by the senators, it wasn't simply because she was a woman. It was because many white men didn't think of her as a woman. The old plantation myths applied to her too. Slave women were thought to be loose, hot and promiscuous, and they couldn't wait to dash from the fields to some big black buck's (or white master's) bed. During slavery, there was no law on the books to protect black women from rape or sexual abuse.

Later, some of the best and brightest black actresses and entertainers paid their dues playing sultry harlots, whores and tramps who hopped from bedroom to bedroom. Nina Mae McKinney bumped and grinded on the dance floor in *Hallelujah*. Lena Horne pranced around in *Cabin in the Sky* tempting the fellows. Dorothy Dandridge was an amoral gold digger in *Carmen Jones*. Fredi Washington in *Imitation of Life* was the tragic mulatta suspended between two worlds. White men in those days could never love or accept her as a true woman especially if they believed she spent her life in a perpetual hunt to do the "wild thang."

NOTE: In those days? I'm not making this up. My publisher offered to send Woman's Day Magazine a review copy of my new

*book, <u>Black Fatherhood II: Black Women Talk About Their Men.</u>
The book features interviews with five black women on family, love
and relationships. It was endorsed by Terry McMillan. This was
the reply. "Great idea for a book, but <u>Woman's Day</u> is aimed
exclusively at women! "*

Anita really shouldn't have had to worry. Black women
don't have the monopoly on dirty images. Tell me how
many of the workmates in the stable of Hollywood superstar
madam Heidi are black women? Most of the high priced
prostitutes are white. They don't ply their trade on the
streets but in expensive salons and mansions. They rarely
get busted because their clients are some of the richest, most
powerful men in America. Unlike black women, they don't
call the women that service them whores or tramps, but
madams, call girls, escorts and professionals.

The same goes for welfare. Many white Americans take
it as an article of faith that lazy, irresponsible black women
lay around all day in the ghetto making babies with lazy,
irresponsible black men and then run to the welfare office
and expect public tax dollars to take care of them. If I said
that far more lazy, irresponsible white women lay around all
day in backwash, rural towns making babies with lazy,
irresponsible white men, and then run to the welfare office
and expect public tax dollars to take care of them, some
would suggest I need a psychiatric attendant. While neither
stereotype is true, white women do make up the bulk of the
welfare recipients.

*NOTE: This was buried at the end of a short news story on
poverty in California "Yuba County had the highest teen-age birth
rate of any county in California." Blacks alone can't be blamed
since they comprise only 4.2 percent of the County's population.*

"Facts are stubborn things," said Ronald Reagan in 1988. I know quoting Reagan is overkill but here I couldn't resist.

III

While Anita made it close for Deh Judge, she didn't win. Diseree Washington did. She had some things going for her that Anita didn't. She didn't wait for nearly a generation to accuse Mike Tyson of sexually abusing her. She was in Indiana, a state more Southern than Northern. She was young, apparently innocent and a beauty queen. Iron Mike wasn't a staid, conservative politically connected black man. He was big, black, brawny Iron Mike, the modern-day reincarnation of Bad Nigger Jack Johnson. Tyson was a Brooklyn street tough, ex-thief, reform school bully and wife beater. He had a lengthening rap sheet that included car wrecks and sexual assaults. What sane person couldn't believe that Tyson couldn't commit rape. RAPE!

His only hope was to throw himself on the mercy of history. Following emancipation, Southern states gradually put rape laws on their books. Theoretically, they applied to black women too. But, everyone knew better. For nearly a century, there were few cases of any white man being convicted of raping a black woman. To this day, there is absolutely no record of any white man being executed for raping a black woman. And there never will be.

The Supreme Court decision in 1967 no longer made rape a capital crime (unless there is a murder). Two years later a Florida court finally sentenced a white man to life imprisonment for the rape and murder of a black woman. This didn't necessarily mean that the law or public opinion had become any more enlightened.

A black co-ed was assaulted and raped at St. Johns University in 1991 by three white students. In a feature story, the *New York Times* agonized over the white student's plight. It quoted extensively the defense attorneys, played up the solid middle-class background of the students and parents, and dismissed the defendant in one line as "dropped out of St. Johns after the incident." INCIDENT? It was a rape case! There was only a brief quote from the prosecutor, and no comments from her friends or relatives. The year before a white woman was "wilded" by young blacks in Central Park. Just for fun check out the *Times* coverage of that case. See any differences?

Tyson could pray that the court would remember that black women for most of this century weren't thought of as real women, but whores. If he had been the average brother and Washington the average sister, he might have skipped away scot-free. If he had been a politically, well-heeled white man like William Kennedy Smith he would have skipped away scot-free. But, he was Iron Mike.

In defending himself against Anita during the confirmation hearings, Deh Judge explained the problem he and Iron Mike had. "If you want to track through this country in the Nineteenth and Twentieth Century the lynchings of black men, you well see that there is invariably a relationship with sex, an accusation a person can't shake off."

Deh Judge wasn't through, "I cannot shake off these accusations because they play to the worst stereotypes we have about black men in this country." Feminists and civil rights leaders went ape. To them, it was blasphemy for him to compare what Anita said about him to a lynching:

a) He was an "Uncle Tom."
b) It was self-serving, cynical and opportunistic.
c) Anita was not a white woman or a lynch mob.
d) He was still alive.

Deh Judge still had a point. Black men weren't lynched

because they raped white women. In many cases they weren't even accused of a crime. Black men were lynched for the same reason they were demonized as lazy, irresponsible, sex-crazed brutes and defectives; to maintain white control, power and domination. Rape was a serviceable myth. And Southerners joyfully reminded everyone that black men were brutes toward their own women too. That was Deh Judge's problem. It was Iron Mike's too.

IV

The myth of rapacious black male sexuality is still one of white America's most durable and deadly stereotypes. Contrary to popular view, it far predated the Atlantic Slave Trade. In the early 1500s, European explorers in West Africa were fascinated with black sexual practices. One explorer called the penises of Mandingo tribesmen "burthensome members." Another marveled at their "large propagators." Later Shakespeare couldn't resist talking about those "lustful" darkies. The black Othello had goo goo eyes for the white Desdomona. As such, she was always in grave danger from "the gross clasps of a lascivious Moor."

The white planters didn't have to read Shakespeare to figure out they needed more than whips, guns, laws, slave patrols, dogs and the militia to keep the darkies in line. They needed a myth, one that they could elevate to national hysteria. Black hyper-sexuality was perfect. They convinced themselves and most whites that those bestial black men with their large propagators were after their dainty white women.

For a time during slavery, North Carolina, Pennsylvania, New Jersey and Virginia even stuck a few laws on their books proscribing castration for any black man that attempted to rape a white woman. They quickly erased the laws. It had nothing to do with stricken consciences. Too many blacks running around with loped off private parts were damaged goods and bad for business.

Defeat in the Civil War didn't change much. Southern politicians and the former planters working under the cover of the KKK and other white supremacist organizations launched a successful campaign of racial terrorism that rolled back the meager Reconstruction gains. When they finished, blacks were free in name only. To make sure it stayed that way, they revived the old myth that the bestial black men with "large propagators" were after white women. Southern newspapers and magazines were filled with lurid, unsubstantiated accounts of white women being threatened by black men.

The politicians got into the act. In 1900, Clifton Brekinridge, diplomat and U.S. minister to Russia, issued this dire warning to the nation about the black race, "When it produces a brute, he is the worst and most insatiate brute that exists in human form."

The learned men weren't far behind. They had already made their compelling case for black inferiority, now they took dead aim at black hyper-sexuality. In 1903, Dr. William Lee Howard triumphantly announced in *Medicine* that the "brutes were driven to fits of sexual madness" because of "the large size of their penis." Unlike the white man's penis, the Doc assured, the black brute's penis lacked "the sensitiveness of the terminal fibers." Skip the mumbo jumbo, the learned man was simply saying that no women were safe from black men with their massive, throbbing dicks.

Howard was not a quack. His colleagues did not challenge his theories. In fact, forty years later they were still trying to prove them. In 1942, the renowned scholar William Montague Cobb in the *American Journal of Physical Anthropology* produced five studies including his own that purportedly proved that black men had bigger penises than white men. Mercifully, Cobb didn't mention anything about "sensitive terminal fibers." The meaning was still the same. Women watch out!

NOTE: The initiation process in this kind of thinking often starts early. Two white boys were joking about sex. I was standing nearby. Suddenly, one turned to the other, pointed to me, and said, "let's ask him about doing it. They know all about that stuff." I was in the sixth grade.

Laugh if you will. Americans took these men seriously. During those years, thousands of black men dangled from trees, were roasted on bonfires, or riddled with bullets because of the theories of the learned men, the ravings of politicians and the fears of the public. This was the extra-curricular stuff. When the mobs played out, the states took over. From 1930 to 1981, 455 men were executed for rape, of that number, 405 were black men. They were put to death on the flimsiest evidence, mostly the word of a white woman. It was nice and legal then, and it still is today.

In Dallas, researchers noted that the rape of a white woman brings a sentence that averages ten years, a black woman two years. This doesn't just happen in hang-em-high Texas. The findings have been duplicated in dozens of other states. The issue is not income or gender, but race.

NOTE: Remember U.S. Supreme Court Justice Roger Taney's famous dictum in the Dred Scott case in 1857 that a black man has no rights that a white man is bound to respect? Well, I was curious. If black life was so devalued and white life so elevated, were there ANY cases where whites were ever executed for killing blacks?

Watt Espy studied 15,978 legal executions since 1608. He found thirty cases where whites were put to death for killing blacks.

The percent is a paltry .00188 percent of the total.

Ahh, now get your calculator out and put your finger on the subtract key because there are some kickers. Subtract the seven victims who were slaves (property, not human beings). Subtract several other murderers who were foreigners. Subtract the ones who had committed other murders (white victims). The rest were the scuzziest of low lifes. But they were white. You can keep them in, but you still must move the decimal point a couple of more places left. In any case, no white man has been executed for killing a black in the past half century.

V

It took time, but Iron Mike finally figured all this out. He said in an interview from prison in 1993, "Michael Jackson and Michael Jordan—like myself and many other black entertainers and celebrities with high profiles—are under attack and every black in the world should offer support. White society hates us just as much as they hate ordinary blacks."

That's why many black women rallied behind Deh Judge and, to some extent, sympathized with Tyson. They understood that the issue is first and foremost race. Civil rights leaders and feminists dodged this. They claimed that the black women who doubted Anita and had reservations about Washington, were brainwashed by men, full of self-hate or simply didn't grasp the "complexity" of the issues.

They refused to face the painful truth that many working class black women reject feminism because they're suspicious of white women. They see feminism as a movement of, by and mostly for middle-class, white women. They know many don't accept them as equals or fight hard against racism. The black feminists should know this. They talk themselves blue in the face trying to get feminist organizations to fight hard for issues that impact black women and other women of color.

Those issues go way beyond the issue of sexual harassment. In America, race, not gender, has always been the driving force behind black female oppression. Black women were captured, shackled in slave ships, suffered illness, starvation and fed to sharks during the Middle Passage because of race, not gender. Black women were worked, sold, beaten and killed during slavery, because of race, not gender. Black women were lynched, burned, shot and beaten during the lynching era because of race, not gender. Black women were relegated to poverty, peonage and ghettos because of race, not gender. Today, black women make less, and are treated worse then anyone else in America because of race and gender.

Louise D. Stone knew this, "There are two kinds of females in this country—colored women and white ladies, and the only time they become ladies is when they are cleaning ladies."

Feminists wage passionate battles for abortion, but not for domestic wages, welfare rights, increased funding for jobs, skills and educational training for black and poor women. Where would Anita be today if, instead of beating up on Deh Judge, she demanded: more funding and expanded programs for family planning clinics; more treatment facilities and better quality care for mothers and infants who suffer alcohol, crack and AIDS related diseases; fair pay and equal rights for domestics; and, wages for housework?

Where would she be if she crusaded for the press and police to take seriously the incessant serial killing of black and poor women; stronger police action; and, laws that punish rapes and physical assaults on black women (by white and black men)? Would the feminists trot her around the country, heap hefty speakers fees and awards on her? Would they call her the Ida B. Wells of the Nineteenth Century or the Rosa Parks of the 1990s?

Feminists and civil rights leaders waged war against Deh Judge before he wrote one opinion, yet turned into deaf mutes on the unholy Richard Nixon-Reagan Trinity of Supreme Court Justices Anton Scalia, William Rehnquist and Anthony Kennedy who wrote dozens of opinions savaging civil rights, civil liberties protection, women's rights and abortion.

NOTE: Here's how silly it got during the Thomas confirmation hearings. A prominent black female California state senator while raging against Deh Judge declared she'd rather see a white racist on the bench than Thomas. Better a white reactionary foursome, then a Technicolor reactionary foursome, I guess.

Black women don't have to be feminists to fight against sexual abuse and for equal rights, equal respect and dignity. The best proof is Hill and Washington. Pre-Deh Judge, Anita had no problem calling herself a Republican and conservative. Washington was prancing around the stage in Indianapolis in a skimpy bathing suit with dozens of other black women trying to cop the Miss Black America crown. Feminists hate these events. They claim these pageants turn women into fetishes, commodities and sex objects.

There's something else feminists and civil rights leaders refuse to admit about blacks, men and women. They are basically conservative. I'm not talking about the political pandering of black conservatives such as Shelby Steele, Thomas Sewell or Deh Judge.

I'm talking about conservative in their values and ideals. They have been thoroughly shaped (OK, for the radicals indoctrinated) by the American experience. Forget what the racists say. From slavery to the present, hard work, thrift, religion, family values, business and self-help have been trademarks of Black America. Blacks are America's most native sons and daughters. The blood of their sons and daughters has drenched every domestic and foreign battlefield. They have rejected all "isms," including communism, socialism, progressivism, Peace and Freedom partyism and Libertarianism.

They have been among the biggest cheer leaders for the two party system. When *Black Enterprise Magazine* asked blacks "if their hopes and aspirations were the same as the white middle class" sixty-one percent said "yes." The only reason more didn't agree is because despite all the faith of their fathers, America eternally finds nasty little ways to remind black folks that they are still "niggers."

NOTE: It was radical chic during the 1960s for black and white revolutionaries to anoint the black masses "the revolutionary vanguard." I, and many others, listened to them, believed them and got into trouble. We should have listened and believed our parents and grandparents. They were neither revolutionary, nor the vanguard. They always talked about religion, country, moral values and basic rights. Period. They were the true bellwether of what black folks really thought.

The forty or so academics and activists that *Black Scholar* magazine in 1992 invited to speak out on Anita and Deh Judge, generally missed most of this. They skirted the issues of conservatism, black resistance and/or indifference to feminism, racism in the women's movement, black male sexuality myths and class divisions among blacks. The majority of them bashed Deh Judge because his views were wildly out of line with the "civil rights-progressive" agenda, in short, theirs.

Politically, I and Deh Judge are intergalactic light years apart. I can challenge his views and protest his abominable rulings. But I don't have the right to tell him he can't have those views. The black critics don't either. When they do they become thought police, self-appointed guardians of truth.

The truth is that many black men and women, for better or worse, have more in common with Deh Judge and Tyson (and mainstream American thinking), than with feminists and academics.

These blacks didn't pay much attention to the intellectual theorists. They knew intuitively that something was wrong. They knew that the system was treating these two black men differently. This is why they didn't believe Anita.

6

Ain't I a Nigger Too

"I don't mind someone calling me a nigger if they call me to go to lunch too." I knew comedian Paul Mooney was trying to get a laugh when he said that. After all, his job is to make people laugh and normally he succeeds. That afternoon, I appeared with Paul and two other black writers on a popular radio talk show in Los Angeles. The subject was racial hate words.

When Paul, who loudly declared that he is not offended when whites call him a nigger, made his little joke, the other two blacks laughed. I didn't. Maybe I was feeling a little too "sensitive" that day (Isn't that what some white folks tell blacks when they object to a racist slur?). I was thinking about the conversation I had with my son a week earlier. I had heard him greet one of his buddies who had called with, "Yo nigger, what's up."

It wasn't the first time that I heard him say that to one of his friends. In the past I ignored it. I knew it was the way many young blacks talked to each other. The word nigger is part of their hip jargon. They aren't particularly troubled by the odious significance of the word. This time I was. I asked him why he used it. He shrugged and said that everybody uses it. "If that's true," I asked, "then what if one of your white friends calls you a nigger?" "Is that OK?" He was silent.

We both knew that it was not acceptable for a white person to call him a nigger. When any white person, especially a celebrity or public official, slips and uses the word or makes any other racist reference, they'll hear about it from outraged blacks. Ask Cincinnati Reds owner, Marge Schott, and sports personalities, Al Campanis and Jimmy "the Greek" Snyder.

The double standard that my son and other young blacks apply to whites, but reject for themselves, is now coming back to haunt them. Many young whites, like blacks, casually toss the word around.

Not long ago, a friend found out how casually. He and two young whites were in an elevator. Suddenly, one of the whites jokingly called his friend a nigger. It didn't matter to him that a black man was standing there. Was it racism? Was it cultural insensitivity, or just plain ignorance on his part? Did he realize that many blacks find the word offensive?

Probably not. He was dressed in the latest baggy style. In the cross-over world of hip culture, he's almost certainly heard many blacks call other blacks, nigger. I'm also pretty sure that he's heard black comedians and rappers sprinkle the word throughout their rap lyrics and comedy lines. Rapper Easy E has virtually made a fetish out of the word. He put it in the title of one song and then rode it to the top of the record charts.

Some black writers go through lengthy gyrations to justify using the word. Their rationale boils down to this, the more a black person uses the word, the less offensive it becomes. They claim that they are cleansing the word of its negative connotations so that racists can no longer use it to hurt blacks. Comedian, turned activist, Dick Gregory had the same idea some years ago when he titled his autobiography, *Nigger*. Black writer, Robert DeCoy also tried to apply the same racial shock therapy to whites when he titled his novel, *The Nigger Bible*.

Many blacks say they use the word endearingly or affectionately. They say to each other, "You're my nigger if you don't get no bigger." Or, "that nigger sure is something." Others use it in anger or disdain, "Nigger you sure got an attitude." Or, "A nigger ain't shit." Still, others are defiant. They say they don't care what a white person calls them, words can't harm them. Funnyman Paul Mooney doesn't have a problem with this.

Black folks miss the point. Words are not value neutral. They express concepts and ideas. Often, words reflect society's standards. If color-phobia is one standard, then a word, as emotionally charged as nigger, can easily reinforce and perpetuate stereotypes. The word nigger does precisely that. It is the most hurtful and enduring symbol of black oppression.

II

Nigger derives from the Spanish word *negro* or black. Its original root is the Latin word, *Niger*. Historian, Winthrop Jordan, in *White Over Black* traces the history of Western attitudes toward blacks. He makes a compelling case that even before the slave trade, Europeans considered anything black, repugnant.

The *Oxford Dictionary* defines black as, "soiled, dirty, foul, malignant, sinister, horrible, wicked, a sign of danger and repulsion." White is defined as "purity, virtue and honor." In Shakespeare's *Othello*, Emilia groans to Othello, "O, the more angel she / And you the blacker devil."

The early European traders and explorers in Africa filled their diaries and journals with weird tales about the supposed animalistic and heathen practices of the Africans. To them, the black Africans were an alien people. It was only a short step from this, to calling them subhuman. This provided the slave trader the mental margin needed to debase blacks and turn them into property. In Western language and thought, the words "Negro" and "slave" soon became synonymous with degradation, while the words, "Christian," "free," "English" and "white" meant the exact opposite.

The word "nigger" crept into the English language in the Seventeenth Century. In 1625, a Rhode Island law decreed, "there is a common course practised among English men to buy negers, to that end they may have them for service or slaves forever." During slavery, blacks were commodities to be bought, sold and traded for labor and profit. Beyond that, their lives had little value. Supreme Court Justice Roger Taney, in the Dred Scott decision in 1857, was brutally frank when he wrote that Negroes "have no rights that a white man is bound to respect."

OK, so I opened this book quoting Huck's exchange with his Aunt Sally in *Huckleberry Finn*, but I just have to use the quote again since Mark Twain used it to capture the total worthlessness of black lives during slavery. Aunt Sally asked Huck why he was late arriving. Huck lied and told her that his boat had been delayed:.

Huck: "We blowed out a cylinder head."
Aunt Sally: "Good gracious! Anybody hurt?"
Huck: "No'm killed a nigger."

Aunt Sally: "Well it's lucky; because sometimes people do get hurt."

In other words to Aunt Sally, "niggers" ain't people! Emancipation did little to alter this thinking. For nearly a century, "separate but equal" was enshrined in American law and custom and blacks were banished to the outer dimension of American society. When Dr. Martin Luther King led civil rights marches in Chicago in 1966, many whites shouted at him: "I wish I were an Alabama trooper, because then I could kill a nigger legally." King later remarked that he had been called nigger so often by whites in Chicago, he began to wonder if he had a new name. In any case, King certainly knew that his life meant nothing to them.

King's experience was hardly unique. A writer passing a group of white children playfully pelting some black children with rocks, asked one, "Why are you throwing rocks at those children?" The youngster innocently replied, "Mister, they ain't children, they're niggers."

Before World War I, America's major magazines and newspapers continued to treat blacks as social outcasts. Historian Rayford Logan surveyed early issues of *Atlantic Monthly, Century Monthly, North American Review, Harpers, the Chicago Tribune, New York Times, the Boston Evening Transcript, the Cincinnati Enquirer, and the Indianapolis Journal.* The publications didn't just savage black men as clowns, criminals and crazed sex maniacs, they also routinely referred to them as "nigger," niggah," "coon," and "darky."

The NAACP and black newspaper editors waged vocal campaigns against this racist stereotyping. Black scholar, W.E.B. DuBois frequently took white editors to task for refusing to spell "Negro" with an upper case "N." DuBois called their policy a "conscious insult" to blacks. In that era, being called a Negro was a matter of pride and self-identity.

There were more deadly consequences. According to the NAACP, from 1880 to 1968, 3,445 blacks were lynched or burned to death in America. (This is the official figure, many suspect that the number is much greater). For many their only crime was their color.

Black men aren't lynched or burned anymore, but the quantum leap in hate crimes nationally is strong proof that racial violence is hardly a thing of the past. The majority of the attacks are still aimed at blacks. And "nigger" is the favorite racist epithet that vandals plaster on the walls of black homes and businesses.

III

The "N" word has also left psychological scars on past generations of black children who American society treated like racial untouchables. Some years ago, psychologist Edward Weaver asked one hundred elementary school children, "When did you first discover that you were a Negro," some responded:

"At a white neighbor's house the other children drank from a dipper, but when I asked for a drink," she said, "You're a nigger, and we don't allow niggers to drink from that dipper."

"One day a little boy called me a nigger, since then I thought of myself as a Negro and not just another person."

That was the idea. In spite of this, many black folks managed to turn what was intended as a badge of shame into a mark of pride and accomplish great things. This is one reason why we're still here today.

"When I asked for a hamburger in a cafe, the man told me that he was sorry that they didn't serve niggers. This told me that I was a Negro and couldn't act like whites."

Today, that's changed. Blacks can go anywhere and eat all the greasy hamburgers and French fries they want to their heart's discontent. But, the message hasn't changed. They still can't act like whites. Former Washington D.C. mayor Marion Barry forgot that. He thought he could lie, cheat and toke a little white powder. When he got caught, he and some black leaders squawked that white politicians do that and much more and get away with it. If they do get caught, they get hand-slap sentences and are not mauled in the press.

Black leaders should have listened to what the young student said years ago. They can act like white men, but they won't be treated like them. I should add, if they commit crimes, they shouldn't expect to be treated like martyrs either.

Here's another example. In Los Angeles some young brothers acted like the four white cops who beat up Rodney King. They beat up white truck driver Reginald Denny. Three of them languished in jail with extortionate bail, court appointed attorneys, while the press lambasted them as gang bangers, thugs and hoodlums. When the legal dust finally settled, two were placed on probation, the other was sent on a fast track to state prison with the maximum sentence.

With the four cops, the judges bent over backwards to grant them low bail, full legal assistance and favorable rulings. All the while, they busily promoted their books and became media celebrities. A jury with no blacks fully acquitted them in state court.

When two were finally convicted in federal court, the presiding federal judge, John G. Davies, was not willing to concede an inch. He described them and their families in almost idolatrous terms. He ignored the pleas of federal prosecutors to toss the book at them and barely blew a feather light page at them. They will luxuriate at a minimum security federal prison, aptly called "Club Fed."

The young brothers forgot one thing, when they acted like white men, especially the ones that wear uniforms and badges and commit crimes, they won't be treated like white men. Again, I'll add, if they commit crimes, they should not expect to be treated like martyrs either.

NOTE: Question. If former Joint Chief of Staff Chairman Colin Powell, former Los Angeles Mayor Tom Bradley, and yes, even Deh Judge had been tooling around Lakeview Terrace instead of Rodney King that March night, when it came time to kick some black ass, would those cops have made fine distinctions?

Novelist Richard Wright in his memorable essay, "The Ethics of Living Jim Crow," remembers the time he accepted a ride from a "friendly" white man. When the man offered him a drink of whiskey, Wright politely said, "Oh no." The man punched him hard in the face and said "Nigger ain't you learned to say, 'sir,' to a white man." The pain from the blow would pass, but the pain from the "N" word would stay with him forever.

Maybe that's why comedian Richard Pryor told a concert audience that he would never use the word nigger again. The audience was stunned. The irreverent Pryor had practically made a career out of using the word in his routines. Pryor softly explained that the word was profane and disrespectful. He was dropping it because he had too much pride in blacks and himself. The audience applauded. Paul Mooney, Easy E, my son, and anyone else who thinks its hip to call someone a nigger, should go rent the tape of that concert.

7

The Way Things Ought Not To Be

I say megga dittos to Rush Limbaugh for telling whites the truth about the "black problem." This shouldn't be surprising. In fact, for a man who has elevated back alley woofing to national respectability, and gotten away with it, nothing should be a surprise. Big Rush says blacks are in the lousy shape they're in for two reasons. One, "The federal government has assumed the role of the wage earning father" for blacks. Note the juxtaposition of "wage earning" and "father." It bears importantly on the second reason.

Two, "sixty-two percent" of all black babies are born to single black women. The result, "there are no role models for young blacks." Since Big Rush doesn't consider dope dealers, drive-by shooters, gang bangers and derelicts as "role models," black folks, says Big Rush, are stuck with a bunch of pickaninnies running around waiting for the next handout from their Sugar Daddy in Washington.

NOTE: Ignore the "sixty-two percent." According to the 1990 Census, forty-three percent of black homes were single parent households.

As always Big Rush pulls figures from a hat, tosses them out and never cites a footnote or reference to support his point. But, when the subject is irresponsible black men, you don't need to. Everyone knows the only thing they're good at is making babies, problems and freeloading. Big Rush dusted off the century-old myth of the irresponsible, shiftless, lazy darky, spruced it up and spit it back to us.

II

He should thank the government. In 1965, it resurrected the modern-day version of the myth. That was the year Watts exploded, black folks escalated their demands for jobs and justice, and more started listening to Malcolm X's recorded speeches. Lyndon Johnson was at his wits end trying to figure out why blacks could be so ungrateful for all his Great Society munificence. He demanded answers.

Enter Assistant Secretary of Labor, Daniel Patrick Moynihan. Johnson told him to explain their bizarre behavior. Moynihan doggedly studied stats, figures and the charts. Instantly, it became clear. Johnson was barking up the wrong tree. He thought that spending millions on jobs, education, housing, social service programs and passing civil rights laws could buy social peace. For all the good it did, the government might as well have tossed the money into the black hole.

The real problem, said Moynihan, was the black family. It was a wreck. Moynihan figured that one in four homes were without fathers. The black single mothers left to fend for themselves were getting poorer and more desperate. All the health, education and welfare programs in the world couldn't change that. Just get those daddies back in the home and everything would be fine.

But, three out of four fathers were in the home. And, many of those were desperately poor homes, too. Moynihan didn't explain why. Many blacks wondered about his research methods that pointedly fingered black men as the root of "Negro deviancy." They asked, did Moynihan control for income, education, professional and family background to make sure that he was comparing middle-class blacks to middle-class whites? Or, did he skew the numbers by comparing ALL blacks to the white middle class? When black family experts put controls in, they found absolutely no differences between the father absenteeism rates in white and black middle-class families.

NOTE: Here's an intriguing project for a sociology grad student. Collect income, welfare and household stats on poor whites and compare them with the income, welfare and household stats of the black middle class and see how poor whites stack up on poverty and father absenteeism.

This might have spoiled Moynihan's hypothesis. Social scientists always hate that. Still, there was just enough doubt raised about the report that Johnson decided to table it. But, the media didn't. With Vietnam turning into a quagmire, black radicals screaming "get whitey," and cities from Detroit to San Francisco burning, the story of black family dereliction was just too good to pass up.

III

By the 1980s, the Reagan revolution had kicked into high gear and the nation's racial mood turned even uglier. The media decided the time was right to resurrect the old derelict, darky myth again to explain the growing army of black poor. Soon, the airwaves and newspapers throbbed with gloomy stories about the "Vanishing Black Family." Much of the media didn't dwell too much on the economic devastation caused by Reaganism. A good story to editors is like a hypothesis to the scientists, they don't want it spoiled.

One thing, however, should spoil it. The great communicator stripped away job, housing and education programs. He sabotaged unions and deepened the rust on the traditional auto, steel, rubber and oil refining plants that provided high paying, union secured jobs for many blacks. Before that, black men did not have a chronic unemployment rate double that of white males. And, young black males did not have a triple or higher unemployment rate than young white males. The majority of black men were in the home.

But, Reagan didn't screw things up by himself. Many state and local officials dutifully took their cue from Washington and imposed iron clad income limits on welfare recipients. If there was a man in the house and he brought in dollars, no matter how meager, the family in the eyes of welfare bureaucrats looked like Rockefellers and Vanderbilts. Their payments were slashed or cut-off entirely. It might have been cheaper to keep her, but it wasn't cheaper to keep him. The doors in many black homes started to revolve and some black men marched out.

That in itself did not cause the black family to plunge into hopeless ruin. There was never any hard evidence that boys raised in one parent families were being groomed as high school drop-outs, drive-by shooters, dope dealers and gang bangers. If some were, it was not because of absentee fathers, but because of absentee income.

Also, many black men who did abandon the home did not entirely abandon their children. A few honest researchers found that black men are far more likely to acknowledge their children, visit them frequently, and provide some money, clothes and food for them. This in part explains why far fewer black women throw themselves on the mercy of the court to collect alimony and child support than white women. (The other part is racism in the legal system.)

There is something else. Black guys aren't the only ones vanishing from homes. A lot of white guys are, too. The days when Ozzie could stroll home after a hard day at the office and expect to be greeted by a beaming Harriet, with apron, smile, slippers, dinner on the table and a spic and span house are dead. That's because American society has undergone profound technological, social and economic changes. This has radically changed the family (especially women). Women have to work. Many are better educated, hold jobs in higher professions, make more money and are independent. Even if they wanted to, and many don't, they wouldn't have the time to be cheerful house wives. They expect and demand that men pull their share.

NOTE: Do you really believe that every white American family resembled Ozzie and Harriet during the "golden fifties?" If you do, I have a rain forest in the Gobi desert to sell to you. Ozzie was an authoritarian who badgered Harriet, spent virtually no time with David, and brow beat Ricky. Writer David Halberstam understood exactly why Ricky later in life battled through a wrecked marriage and drug problems. He was the "unhappy product of a dysfunctional family." In the Fifties, Halberstam tells all about the All-American fraud of Ozzie and Harriet.

IV

Maybe I should pardon Big Rush for being a little ignorant of this history, some of this happened before his time. But,

Big Rush should take a break from horsing around with his chums at the Institute of Advanced Conservative Studies, leave the friendly confines of his studio and drive through any black neighborhood. He can do it at high noon on the weekend. The muggers don't operate as well at that hour. He should look past the guys hanging out on the corners and go to a park, playground, cultural event or church activity. He will see many black men with their wives or significant others and children at play, work or just relaxing.

Who are these guys? They are barbers, plumbers, teachers, electricians, doctors, lawyers, accountants, engineers, policeman, mailmen, firemen and so on. They want the same thing for their children that white fathers want, a better life.

This might be too burdensome for Big Rush. In his mega-seller, *The Way Things Ought To Be*, Big Rush spent considerable time trying to resuscitate Ronald "my hero" Reagan from Sleepy Hollow. Big Rush thinks he's the true people's champion. He is the man on the perennial white horse who rescued America from the Satanic clutches of the "liberals."

Then there's the Limbaugh Lexicon, a dimwitted collection of Limbaughisian slop, complete with racist and sexist code words, stock lines and idiotic slogans. Buried in this mess, Big Rush mentions only four men. I already told you who one is. Another, New York Governor Mario Cuomo is there for reference. The other two are black men, Jesse Jackson and "General" Dinkins, better known as former New York Mayor David Dinkins. The "General" is dispatched quickly as the "hapless" ineffective mayor of New York," a tool of every liberal group one can think of." In other words this ignorant darky couldn't have bumbled through his four years as mayor without help from white carpetbaggers. (Southerners hated carpetbaggers. They were considered the liberals of their day.) Big Rush kills two birds with one stone here.

And then there's the good Reverend. Big Rush is a little sneakier here. He doesn't take Jackson on directly. He does that in many other places in the book. He pokes fun at him for the way he talks. Now, Jesse does sometimes do strange things with the King's English, but so do a lot of white folks in high places. This includes, if I remember correctly, his own "hero." But, that's different. White folks don't speak "black English" like "those people."

Oh well, this is a good place to leave Big Rush with a few lines from Dr. Andrew Billingsley, who studied Census data and does cite sources. "A majority of African-Amercans live in households; a majority of these are family households; a majority of family households are married couple households."

Since Billingsley is not a "ditto-head," Big Rush will pooh-pooh talk like that. If he didn't, he could never tell anybody, "see, I told you so."

8

Minister Farrakhan or Adolph Farrakhan?

I know what Adolph Hitler and the Nation of Islam leader, Louis Farrakhan, have in common: Jews. For nearly a decade, Jewish organizations have branded him the "black Hitler." How did Farrakhan beat out George Lincoln Rockwell, the original Mr. American Nazi, for this dubious distinction? Why does his name conjure up gruesome visions among Jews of burning flesh, Zyklon B gas, firing squads, open pits and emaciated bodies in death camps? Could a black man in America have that much diabolical power? Farrakhan doesn't and never will in America. And, many Jewish organizations know it.

II

Blacks assume that many Jews hate Farrakhan because he criticized Jewish organizations and religious practices in his speeches. There's more.

Jewish organizations don't regard Farrakhan as simply a

raving anti-Semite. He's also the symbol of Jewish rage against blacks. Jews are mad because they feel betrayed. They worked hard to build SNCC and CORE during the 1960s. They gave money, time, resources and advice during the civil rights movement. They mourned Michael Schwerner and Andrew Goodman who gave their lives in Mississippi for black freedom. They fought to break down barriers for blacks in unions and corporations.

They are mad because after doing all this, blacks kicked them out of their organizations, denounced Israel, supported the PLO, called them racists and ghetto exploiters and accused them of manufacturing plots and conspiracies. The Minister was the ultimate insult. Since many blacks liked his message, Farrakhan became the symbol of their rage.

But, the rage against him has become a fixation. Many Jews mistakenly view the black experience through the prism of Europe. They forget that the pogroms, Bunds, pales of settlement, Cossack, peasant persecutions and Nazi death camps were products of the ancient European hatred and fear of Jews. The black experience is shaped by the whip, the cross and the rope of American bigotry. Blacks have never had the power nor the desire to oppress or exploit Jews. Their fight has been for justice and empowerment. When a black man preaches the message of empowerment, many blacks will embrace him no matter who it angers.

III

A perfect example is Los Angeles, September 12, 1985. When Farrakhan came to Los Angeles, Jewish leaders, politicians and the press fumed, threatened, cajoled and denounced him. They also denounced Mayor Tom Bradley and local black leaders for not denouncing him. The *Los Angeles Times* in a pompous editorial raked Farrakhan over the coals for "vicious bigotry," "raw racism," and "destructive religious intolerance."

NOTE: The Times admitted that the audience applauded loudest when Farrakhan "reached out to the Jewish community with a word of conciliation." To dwell on this would have blown their script.

This guaranteed a huge gate. Farrakhan was a black man under attack. Instead of the usual 7,000 or 8,000; 16,000 people showed up. Farrakhan served his purpose that day. He was the Blackman that personified all evil. That's all the press allows Americans to see and hear about Farrakhan. They believe that he exists to trash Jews.

There's something they don't see. Fast forward eight years to October 1993. Farrakhan was again in Los Angeles for a major speech. He talked exclusively about building peace between the black gangs and stopping black-on-black fratricide. The message was positive and supportive. He did not mention the word "Jew" once. There was no opportunity to demonize him. Jewish leaders, politicians and the press ignored him.

Farrakhan can't win. He symbolizes the hateful black man who stirs hidden paranoid fears in many whites about blacks. Mention the name Hitler and it touches deep revulsion. Mention the name Farrakhan and it does the same. It's the perfect match made in hell.

9

Why Are They Waiting to Exhale?

I know why Shahrazad Ali's *The Black Man's Guide to Understanding the Black Woman* touched a nerve in many black men. Many black women thought it was because black men got perverse joy out of hearing the sisters dogged by a sister. Some black men did go into delirium when they heard a black woman call black women bossy, pushy, domineering, gold diggers, gossips, backbiters, whiners, disrespectful and sex connivers. Some brothers had a hearty laugh when Ali said the sisters were lousy housekeepers, unkempt and wore dirty braids.

This was strong stuff and it needed a response. When a good friend asked me to appear as part of a men's panel to publicly "confront" Ali during her first visit to Los Angeles, I immediately agreed. I figured that the sister would get a hot reception from the audience. I was ready for her. At her appearance, Ali made it clear beforehand that she would take no part in direct debate. The men could make their case after her lecture and the question period.

An all black crowd packed Patriotic Hall in South Central Los Angeles for her talk. In the lobby, there were vendors hawking books, posters, food and the usual assortment of paraphernalia.

Ali arrived a half hour late in a chauffeur driven Rolls Royce. She was impeccably coifed; and, being the righteous Muslim sister that she is, dressed in a flowing white dress. When she took the stage, she got a loud ovation. After forty or so minutes of a rambling discourse, she took questions. I thought this was where she would get her comeuppance. A few sharply challenged her, but, surprisingly, most didn't. The men, and a large number of women, praised the book. At the end, many in the audience gave her a standing ovation.

When we took the stage, the mood turned ugly. Some of the brothers gave us dagger looks. They had come loaded for hide, ours. One of the brothers who had agreed to participate suddenly couldn't be found.

My friend who had organized the panel spoke first. He barely got a few words out of his mouth when the brothers laid into him with boos and catcalls. He gamely tried to make his points but it was no use. They didn't want to hear any criticism of Ali.

My turn. I scrambled. I gave the standard "we're all in the struggle together" pitch. It sounded weak and lame. I didn't get any catcalls, just silence. I watched the audience file out. They were chuckling and slapping hands. Ali had told them what they wanted to hear and they were happy. In a way, so was I.

II

From slavery to the present, the black man listened to white men savage, twist, malign, libel, batter and mug him in conversation, books and the press. It was painful, but, at least, he understood it. He told himself that white men feared, envied and despised him. Or, he rationalized it by saying "it's a man's thing." By that he meant, white men viewed the black man as a competitor and potential challenger to his power and control.

But now black women were bad mouthing him, too. That he couldn't understand. Ali was his revenge. Her book was his weapon to hit back at them. What made him so mad that he giddily embraced Ali's *Guide* as his guide?

Books. TV talk shows. Newspaper articles. Movies. Everywhere he turned black women were talking about him. The things they said about him sounded suspiciously like the same things white men said about him.

Michele Wallace launched the attack in the early 1970s with her book, *Black Macho and the Myth of the Superwoman.* Wallace claimed that black men's obsession with white women bordered on the clinical. The woman took special delight in downing the men of the Black Power movement. To her, they were a bunch of phonies that used the movement as a cover to satisfy their lust for white women.

What could you say to this? She gave no figures or data on interracial marriage, dating patterns or even bed hopping to back this up. It was one woman's bitter opinion, nothing more. Black men panting after white women. It got a lot of play.

Then there was Ntozake Shange's *Colored Girls*. Shange introduced us to Willie Beau. He was an irresponsible, loathsome drunk who pissed on himself and wallowed in his vomit. He hated his woman (and himself) so much that he threw his own kids out the window.

During the 1980s, the "new era" black women writers stepped up the attack. They styled themselves as tough, no bull shit, take no prisoner sisters ready to smash "the code of silence" about sexism and tell the raw truth about black men.

They wrote books. Gloria Naylor's *The Women of Brewster Place* introduced four black women. Not one had a real man. They had to suffer through guys who were mostly liars, unstable ego maniacs, dick grabbers, pussy chasers and gang rapists. One woman doggedly tried to make a go of it with her man. For her efforts, she was ignored, cursed out and whacked. When he finally decides to walk out, she begs him to stay, pleading "I love you." He rewards her devotion by gruffly telling her, "Well that ain't good enough." BAM.

Alice Walker's *Color Purple* finally drove some black men to revolt. Alice named her black man simply, "Mister." "Mister" was anyman. He was a misogynist, tyrant, abuser, child beater and wife batterer. Even though he saw the light and became a better man at the end of the story, the damage had been done. "Mister" would be remembered as a brute.

Black men cried foul and accused Walker of savaging them. E.T. Spielberg didn't care one way or another that Hollywood never seemed to find a black man who didn't shoot, beat, drink, snort or screw his way across the screen, *Color Purple* sounded like a good yarn to him. And since E.T. had made a bundle turning yarns into juvenile other-world fantasies, *Color Purple* became the smash movie hit of the year.

Black men griped even more. But, this was so much sour grapes. Black women rallied to the sister's defense. They told the brothers to quit bellyaching and "change the reality." Black writer Pearl Cleage, who at one time had her own doubts about feminism, said she felt duty bound to defend Walker, Shange and Naylor, "when they were attacked by black men for creating negative images."

NOTE: I was one of their black critics. I never attacked them for creating negative images of black men. I attacked them for creating

*no other kind of image. We can all name black men whose lives
embody positive images. They don't have to be "created."*

III

Still, trying to "change the reality" is a tall order,
particularly, since many black feminists are convinced that
black men like their white brethren gorge themselves at the
trough of "patriarchy." Probably the most politically
articulate is bell hooks. In *Ain't I A Woman*, she dug deep into
history to "prove" that black men were sexist before slavery.
Presumably she referred to male-female relations within
African society before the European conquest. The popular
notion is that the men had many wives. The women cooked,
cleaned, took care of the kids and served the men. Nothing
more.

She made two mistakes. She judged African communal
society by Western standards. African communal society
was not European Industrial society. In feudal Europe,
women were bound by tradition and rights to the baronial
estates. She was both economic producer and care giver. Her
labor was vital to the economic life of the clan or village. The
European industrial revolution changed this. The power of
the industrial bourgeoisie was based on the iron clad rule of
private property, commodity production, unfettered profit
and personal possession. The historic customs, traditions
and duties of women were obliterated. The marriage contract
resembled a property contract. A woman became a personal
possession. Her labor and service were bound to one man, in
one home. In the factory, capitalist dominance became
supreme. In the home, male dominance became supreme.

In African communal society, private property and
commodity production for profit were alien. Women were

not commodities or property objects. They were not bound by a formal contract to serve and perform labor for one man. They were a vital part of the economic and social life of the village or clan. The household was organized to facilitate shared responsibilities for food production, trade and goods management. Women's roles were respected and honored.

The second mistake by hooks. Polygamy is much criticized and much misunderstood. Not all West African societies were polygamous. A sizable number didn't practice it at all. In those that did, men did not simply collect and subjugate women for sex, personal gratification and child breeding. The system evolved mostly out of economic and social necessity. Men had a nasty tendency to get themselves killed in wars, accidents or while hunting.

In a communal society organized on the basis of economic sharing, group, and mutual protection and defense; a bride(s) was integrated into the economic and social life of the male household. There was no "contract." She did not serve him. She served the group. Child care was a shared responsibility.

Ashanti fathers and mothers had equal responsibility for the care, nurturing and raising of their children. There was far more flexibility in gender relations, interchange of work and fewer stigmas attached, than previously thought to men doing so-called "women's work" and women doing so-called "men's work."

Slavery temporarily blurred the gender lines. Black men and women were brutalized, dehumanized stripped of their culture and language. Black men and women were physically, economically and legally powerless to form, build, nurture and defend their families or develop permanent social relationships. The white master was THE only man on the plantation.

Hooks argues that emancipation changed this. She claims black men were in a mad dash to defend male patriarchy and the black family quickly mirrored the white family. Black men worked, paid the bills and made the decisions. Black women raised the kids, did the housework and followed orders. If she stepped out of line she was abused or beaten. Sex was the clincher. Black men, like white men, turned her into a sex slave, while they were free to roam.

But, there is much evidence that the gender roles in black homes have always been more fluid than in white households. Black women worked, and many black men did share in the housework. Black fathers were more involved in nurturing and raising their children than white fathers. Black men and women overwhelmingly agreed that black men were just as likely to be sharers, givers and takers in that order, as black women.

Sex. Sex. Sex. Hooks takes this to the outer limits, "patriarchy makes husbands and lovers rapists in disguise." Put another way, it's impossible for a black man and woman to build a sensitive, caring relationship based on love and mutual respect. Sex will always get in the way and dirty things up. Well, when you construct a straw man argument, no matter how silly or ridiculous it sounds, you can't lose.

Maybe this is why in her later book, *Talking Back*, hooks admits that her editors at South End Press thought *Ain't I A Woman* was "too negative." They asked her to tone it down. She refused. They published it anyway. Why not? She was mostly criticizing black men.

IV

By the 1990s, the attack on black men had turned into a rout. Black women complained bitterly on TV talk shows, in books and magazine articles that they couldn't find "Mr. Right." They were getting more frustrated by the day. Many black women longed for someone to tell the world once and for all about the misery and heartache these louses were causing them. They wanted someone to show them how to exhale again.

Terry McMillan did. In *Waiting to Exhale*, Gloria, Savannah, Bernadine and Robin can't find a good man among the sad sack dysfunctional bunch of dead beats, misfits, drug addicts, alcoholics and insensitive bums they meet. The familiar stereotypes of black men from the past century come crashing together with a vengeance in their lives. The men all slobber over white women (lustful brutes). They are all ready to hit the road Jack at the first sign that the woman wants them to make a commitment (irresponsible, unstable). They wouldn't know how to tell the truth even under penalty of death (conniving, calculating and deceitful). They are lazy, slothful, and will pick a sister's purse or her pants in a minute (immoral, derelict).

There is one functional relationship in the book. A couple, married thirty-nine years, but by the time we meet them, the man is an old broken down mule dying of Alzheimer's disease. His wife does everything for him. The message: The only time a black man needs a black woman is when he's helpless, ready to be put out to pasture, and can't find any other skirt (presumably white) to chase.

Many black women went wild over this stuff, not because it "was only fiction" as some women snapped, but because they believed it was fact. They were THOSE women in the book. Gloria spoke for them when she bitterly complained that "all men cause pain." It was like peeping in on the pages of *True Confessions*. *Waiting* was the new bible for many black women. To quote and discuss it became part of the new chic.

NOTE: The women that I heard rave the most about the book were college-educated, professional, middle-class, black women. Were the men in <u>Waiting</u> *the only kind of men they could find with* *whom they could have relations? If so, what did that say about them? Worse, what did it say about the women in <u>Waiting</u> who at times seemed more preoccupied with the size of a guy's penis than his brains?*

White critics declared *Waiting* the hit of the year. There was much talk of a movie. As I read the reviews and listened to the talk, a little voice kept whispering something in my ear that an old Black Muslim brother told me years ago, "if HE'S for it, beware." The HE to him was the "white devil." To me it's the white, corporate-controlled media.

In the middle of an interview on black parenting I did with a radio station in a small Oregon town, the host suddenly asked me, "Why can't black men get along with their women?" Huh? How did he know that?

This guy lived in a town that hadn't seen a black since the Johnstowne flood, yet this Peeping Tom was snooping into our collective bedrooms and thinking he knew everything about black folks.

Look, Jewish Rabbis are appalled at the low number of Jewish women marrying Jewish men. Would he ask them why they can't get along with each other? Writers Amy Tan and Isabel Allende blister Chinese and Latino men for their domineering, macho abuse of Chinese and Latino women. Would he ask them why they can't get along with each other? Many Korean men have been compelled to go to violence prevention workshops in Los Angeles because they beat and physically abuse their wives. Would he ask them why they can't get along with each other?

For more than a century, white feminists have been denouncing white men for chauvinism. Would HE ask himself why HE can't get along with his woman? But, this small town yokel had no compunction about asking that about black men and women.

Maybe I was reading too much into all this. So I asked a friend who read *Waiting* why she liked it. She said softly, but firmly, "She spoke for the hurt of every woman who got dressed up, ready for a date and the guy didn't show." I resisted mightily the urge to shoot back, "You're right, I do remember the pain I felt when I spent a day washing and polishing my car, getting dressed up, buying flowers and going to pick up my date only to be met at the door by her sister who embarrassedly told me that she had just left."

That would have been schoolyard one-upmanship. It would have been tantamount to me telling an American Indian that life is rougher in the ghetto than on the reservation. I held my tongue, cut my losses and cooled it, secure in the knowledge that I was a man. As we all know, of course, black men can never have relationships that cause them pain. I did, however, decide to write new love scenarios for the ladies of *Waiting*. Here they are.

Robin's boy friend does not take her to meet his dope dealing friends, and later, steal her purse. He takes her to a church social. Afterwards, they have dinner at a restaurant at his expense.

Bernadine's husband doesn't skip off with his pretty young white secretary. They are still happily married.

The "jerk" that Savannah gets to drive her from Denver to Phoenix does not "make a monstrous face" or "wild beast like sounds" while banging her hard at the motel where they stop for the night. In fact, they don't jump in the sack at all. They spend several hours, relaxing at a nearby club, talking about each others lives and their future plans. Later, when he calls and asks her if he can come to her room, she says she's tired. He softly wishes her good night.

Gloria's teen-age son, Tarik doesn't pick girls "who looked white" to date. Instead, he has a steady girlfriend who IS dark-skinned and wears a natural hairstyle.

The older married couple talk exclusively about their years together before he became sick. If we listen closely to them, we might discover some real truths about how to maintain a lasting relationship.

Don't yawn. If we honestly think about it, there are many Savannahs, Bernadines, Robins and Glorias in relationships with black men like that. Men who aren't afraid of commitments, nurture their children, value companionship and want romance with a black woman. I have to specify black woman, since the women of *Waiting* think that black men only want those kind of relations with white women. That's not so.

Ninety-five percent of black men marry black women. Most of the guys that marry white women don't do it because they think these women are Green Goddesses, forbidden fruit or possess mythical status. Nor do they marry them because they are lustful or filled with self-hate. They marry them for the same reason black men marry black women. They share common interests, and they love them.

A DOUBLE NOTE: (1) Interestingly, the black women who habitually say that their personal relationships are rotten are not middle-income, professional women like Savannah, Bernardine, Robin and Gloria. They are lower income, less educated black women. Now if just one of the legion of sociologists who make careers out of studying Negroes would ask poor white women about their relationships, I wonder what they'd say?

(2) Every black woman worried sick that ALL black men want white women should take this test. Think of all the black men you know. Now how many of them exclusively pursue, date, are married to, or spend every waking moment chattering about white women? Don't cheat.

V

A final question. Is there a major New York publisher willing to spend bundles of money to advertise and promote a book about a black man who dons an apron, and does dishes, cooks and serves dinner to his family and reads a bed time story to his son or daughter? My publisher at Middle Passage Press thought so. These are the black men I talk to, and about, in *Black Fatherhood: The Guide to Male Parenting.* Soon after the book was released, my publisher called me excitedly and said that she had just received a call from a major mass paperback New York publisher. They told her they were interested in obtaining reprint rights for the book.

From the type of books I see churned out these days on black male-female relationships, I knew major publishers weren't interested in publishing books about black men who work hard to build positive, meaningful relationships with their children, wives and significant others; minus drugs, alcohol, crime, gangs, violence and abuse. Even if they were, they still wouldn't publish them because they don't believe the reading public would spend a penny to read them.

But she was so excited that I didn't want to say anything to muck up her mood. Weeks went by with no word from the publisher. She wrote letters and made calls. Finally, they told her, sorry, no go.

I still didn't say anything. I thought of the brothers that hated sister Terry's book and loved sister Ali's book. Then, I really knew why. It finally gave them the chance to exhale.

10

No Thriller for Michael Jackson

I hope Michael Jackson has learned his lesson. His wealth, success, fame, Casper the ghost looking bleached skin, nose pinch job, eye shade, straight hair and gyrating hips can't erase two words on his birth certificate, *black male*. He may have forgotten this, but the press didn't. All it took was the unsubstantiated word of a thirteen year old boy that Mike was a child molester and sex abuser to slap him back to reality. The press pounced on him like vultures picking over carrion. The charge was sex molestation. For a black man who makes his living grabbing his crotch before millions, he was done in from the start. The equation looks like this: black man + sex + perversion = guilt.

Jackson and other black men who wind up on the sexual hot seat remind me of the luckless Americans during the McCarthyite purges of the 1950s. Their personal lives were picked apart by congressional inquisitors. They were battered in the press. Their careers and reputations were destroyed. To escape the shame, some fled the country, others committed suicide. All it took was the unsubstantiated charge that they were a Communist, "fellow traveler" or knew someone who was.

It made no difference whether the charge was true. The witch hunters howled for blood. Politicians, the press and the public tried, convicted and condemned the accused. Years later, a lucky few would be vindicated. Some even resumed their careers. But, the damage had been done. The stigma could never be erased.

We look back on those disgraceful years and swear to the high heavens that it could never happen again in America. But it can. Today, being called a Communist may bring laughter, being called a child or sex abuser, however, will damage a career. It began with the child abuse revelations in the McMartin Pre-School case. It gathered steam with the sex abuse charges leveled at Clarence Thomas by Anita Hill. It came full blast when Michael Jackson was accused of both.

The media quickly displayed its magnificent talent for turning trivia and gossip about Jackson into the "big story." So what if the police didn't find anything? So what if no one bothered to do a background check on the accuser and the alleged witnesses? So what if the District Attorney did not immediately press criminal charges? So what if no one cared how many luggage bags Liz Taylor carried on the plane when she went to meet Jackson on his world concert tour?

With Hollywood Madam Heidi, I mean Jackson, the media happily titillated the public with countless "insider" interviews, features and reports on Jackson's alleged shenanigans. It worked. Based on an unsubstantiated charge the press got the tongues of the public wagging.

II

I suppose it was only a matter of time before Jackson

wound up in the docket. He was always ripe for the pickings. Besides being incredibly rich, he's also obsessively reclusive. The press easily turned the privacy he's spent a lifetime guarding into a damning weapon against him. Even when he bowed to the critics, and tried to show he was a real person by venturing an opinion or two, his words came back to haunt him. In 1992, he told *Ebony* Magazine, Children are loving, they don't gossip, they don't complain, they're just open hearted, they're ready for you. They don't judge."

Oh Boy! "What did he REALLY mean by that?" asked a critic for the *Nation* turned amateur psychoanalyst. He frothed at the prospect of discovering something murky and sinister in those stray remarks. Stuff like this probably made Jackson wish he had kept his trap shut and stayed hidden on his ranch.

The bewildered Jackson continued his world tour in a vain effort to keep up the appearance of normality. But, the charges still continued to fly and a lawsuit was filed against him. The case boiled down to Jackson's word against his accuser's. His prospects weren't good. Even though the case was settled out of court, Jackson still loses. The rumors, whispers and doubts will plague him for years.

He isn't alone. Others have suffered the same fate. In 1992, there were nearly three million reported child abuse cases nationally, triple the number a decade ago. Although only ten percent of the cases resulted in criminal prosecutions, many of the accused still paid a price. Undoubtedly many of them were black men.

A good friend was one. He was accused of abuse against his step daughter. He isn't rich or famous like Jackson. So, he was spared the ordeal of a media trial. Still, he was grilled by social workers, the police and a prosecuting attorney. He spent thousands of dollars on legal fees. He lost days from his work for court appearances. All on the unsubstantiated charge made by the child's father who had a bitter grudge against him and his ex-wife. Although, the case was dropped due to insufficient evidence, the memory will haunt him forever.

Still, I say with no hesitation that the authorities are duty bound to flush child sex abusers out of hiding. When the facts clearly warrant it, they must prosecute. The problem is they should have done that all along. My friend, Jackson and countless other black men wind up as suspects for three reasons. One, the legal system ignored child and sexual abuse charges or treated them as nuisance cases for years. Two, they're men. Three, like I said, they're black.

Only after feminist and child advocate groups screamed about society's insensitivity did lawmakers and the courts pass and enforce tougher laws. Yet, in their mad rush to judgment, they did not develop clear definitions and standards that preserved the rights of both victim and accused. Ultimately, this is the best guarantee that child sex abusers will wind up behind bars and stay there.

But as long as the legal lines are clouded, it will be virtually impossible to prevent opportunists from using the child and sex abuse laws for revenge or personal gain. It also gives the press free license to run amok and peddle gossip as fact. Jackson is tragic proof that public witch hunts damage reputations, but do not educate the public about the very serious problem of child and sex abuse.

That's too bad, despite what many think, traditionally, while some black men walked out on their children, they did not physically abuse them. Maybe that's why a perplexed Jackson shook his head, and mumbled, "but I love children, I always have." Until a judge or a jury tells me otherwise, I believe him. That's the American way—at least on paper.

11

What's Love Got To Do With It?
More Than You Think

I wonder how many people bothered to read pages 206-207 in Tina Turner's autobiography, *I, Tina*. She doesn't mess around. In three words, she said what she really thought about men. "I love men." There were no ifs, ands or buts. If ever a woman was entitled to ifs, ands, or buts, it's Tina. Many of us know her story.

For nearly two decades Ike and Tina Turner were hot ticket items. There was Tina swivelling wildly on stage belting out hard driving rhythm and blues songs in that peculiar guttural voice of hers. They were the real deal. You could look at them and practically smell the collard greens, corn bread and ham hocks. You knew they had paid hard dues in some of the raunchiest dives around before they made it to the big time.

What we didn't know was that behind the scenes Tina

caught hell. She was tormented by a possessive, paranoid, coke-addicted bully. Ike beat her with fists, belts, iron cords, hangers and boots to keep her in line. Much of this was shown in the movie about her life. Many, certainly walked out of the theater shaking their heads thinking, "Yeah, what would you expect, that's the way those black guys treat their women."

Tina didn't see it that way. She did not wring her hands, weep and wail about being a battered woman. She was not going to be a symbol, a martyr or a marionette for the cause of feminism. She made no apologies for her years with Ike. She didn't sharpen her knives on Ike's, or black men's hides. She was not a fool in love. Tina had words for the "intellectuals" (her word not mine) who tried to tell her she was. "I don't give a crap what they think. I did what I had to do there."

She had no regrets at giving Ike manicures, pedicures, choosing his clothes, changing his hair style, being there at his beck and call and catering to his every whim and mood. Even if she had been awake for hours, she didn't get out of bed until he did. She did these things not because he wanted it, but because she wanted it. As far as she was concerned, Ike was one man, ONE MAN, not ALL black men. "Although I had a bad relationship, it did not change my feelings about men."

What are those feelings? Let's start with her father. There is only scant mention of him in the movie. But in her book she talks a lot about him. After her mother skipped off, she and her sister lived with him for five years.

NOTE: The movie gave the impression she lived only with her grandmother.

She says he was a man who was a hard worker. He kept

his daughters in food and clothes. He bought a bigger house for them. Eventually, he ran off, too. Tina doesn't say why. Maybe, he felt overwhelmed trying to take care of two teenage daughters without a wife. Maybe, he was frustrated. Maybe, there was another woman. Who knows? Tina hasn't forgotten that he ran off. She was hurt, "I was so mad at my father." This showed that she cared deeply about him. This is her way of acknowledging that he did try. I believe she has forgiven him.

II

Post Ike. Tina is not afraid to say that she wants her men to be masculine. She wants a man who can stand his ground and be firm. She believes that there are clear gender roles and differences between men and women. Tina revels in them. She measures beauty in part by a man's physical strength. For her this is something a man should be proud of. She doesn't run from those feminine distinctions in herself. She sees strength in being a woman "I love every oil, every cream, every bottle of perfume, anything made for women." She doesn't put these things down as fetishes conjured up to feed into men's sexual fantasies, egos or to fatten the profits for the male-run fashion and cosmetics makers.

She loves the wigs, the short dresses and the knit black stockings. The woman exudes sex not as a commodity, but as an expression of personal sensuality. She's a woman in control. A woman who knows her mind and her body and is not ashamed of it.

In the years away from Ike, Tina has done a lot of thinking about relationships. She knows what she wants. While she wants her man to be strong and masculine, she also wants him to "respect me and my strengths as a woman."

Respect. She wants it. She demands it. She deserves it. She's willing to do the things that are necessary to make a relationship work.

She's willing to be there, be caring, be supportive, be attuned to his needs, and be sensitive to his problems. I suspect that she is even willing to go beyond the call of duty for her man. IF, IF, he's willing to respect and appreciate her for that. She's not trying to make him over or recast him. She asks only that he recognize her for what she is and what she has accomplished.

III

In many ways, she reminds me of my mother and the many black women that I knew growing up. They were working class women, basic sisters, who had a vision of life that included the well-being of their families, their husbands and themselves. These women were strong, proud women. They did not believe in belittling their men, or putting them down in front of their friends or their children. They did not see themselves in competition with their men. They wanted to work together to make a better life. They didn't feel that they were sacrificing their identity and integrity. They wouldn't have paid that price.

These women were not cowed by their men. They were not afraid to speak their mind and tell them when they thought they were wrong. There were stormy times. Sometimes, there was abuse, but they never saw themselves as abused women or victims. They also realized, like Tina, that while some black men were brutal and violent toward their women, many acted this way because of their exaggerated and warped sense of what a man should be and what white society would never allow him to be. Some played out the "bad nigger" role and beat the crap out of her.

Some black men still use their women as punching bags mostly because white society continues to make them its punching bag. There are the daily insults, digs, put-downs and frustrations. These men are still taught from the crib that it's risky business for a "nigger" to hit back against whites. In the past, many who did lost their lives or freedom.

But let's be clear, black men have no monopoly on spousal abuse. In a male dominated society the implicit message men of any color or class receive is that "their women" must be controlled by any means necessary, including violence. As for black men specifically, nobody claims their brutal actions toward women are right or justified, only that there is a reason.

Tina understood, "That's why I stayed. I was in control." If she didn't understand, why else would she have sweated through so many nightmare years with Ike? To me, Tina captures the true beauty, strength and essence of womanhood. What's love got to do with it? Everything.

12

The War on Drugs *Is* a War
on Black Males

I wonder why no one listened to William J. Bennett. Here's what the former Bush drug czar said, "The typical cocaine user is white, male, a high school graduate, employed full-time and living in a small metropolitan suburb."

Someone might think that Bennett was snorting the white powder himself. Anyone who watches TV or reads the papers can plainly see that the typical drug user is black, male, a high school drop out, unemployed and hangs out on a squalid ghetto street corner. That's why Chicago Judge Thomas Sumner went into shock when someone told him what Bennett said. "Judging by what I see, I would think the numbers would be totally reversed." The judge must have thought, by golly, those aren't the folks who stand in front of me every day in my court.

But Bennett, the true-blue Reagan conservative and the

man who never met a multi-cultural textbook he liked, was dead right. One of America's worst kept secrets is that the war on drugs is a war on black men. What else could you call it? The 1992 National Household Survey on Drug Abuse revealed that 8.7 million whites used drugs in one month versus 1.6 million blacks. And white high school seniors were far more likely to use drugs than black high school seniors.

The police and many politicians say it isn't racism. They claim that more blacks deal the drugs and create a greater menace to their communities. Not true. A few sociologists didn't just watch TV, they actually talked to the folks who were actually pushing the junk. They found that white males (93 percent) were way more likely to sell drugs than black males (67 percent). They also started using heroin at a much younger age than blacks and continued to use it longer.

It shouldn't be hard to figure out why. They have the money and the connections. They know the suppliers. They do not live in the ghettos. They are less likely to be arrested. In candid moments some police officials admit they bust more blacks than whites. It's easier. They're all over the streets, oodles of them. They might as well have a sign hanging on them, "Arrest Me." It's numbers man, just numbers! The whites? Many are inside the cozy confines of suburban apartments or high rise offices.

NOTE: What would the public think if the police every night took a live TV action camera crew with them and knocked down those suburban doors?

Think about the time, effort, personnel and resources it takes to find, surveil and build an air tight case against the big boys. Even when they nail them, they may not make the charges stick. Well-connected dealers know how to twist the law and if they don't they'll find lawyers who do.

If they succeed in getting white dealers off the streets there's no guarantee the public will know about it. The Director of the Massachusetts Division of Alcohol and Drug Rehabilitation confessed that when whites are busted the police were respectful of the families wishes about "bad" publicity. They were more than happy to help them keep their problems out of the press. I'd add this. The press probably wouldn't care anyway unless the white person busted happened to be named Madonna, Ronald Reagan or Bill Clinton.

The image of young blacks proned out on the ground, handcuffed against walls and over the hoods of police cars makes better copy anyway. TV can get its action photos for the nightly news. The dailies can recycle their customary drug hysteria-in-the-ghetto-story. Police can keep their arrest numbers up. Politicians can prattle about tougher laws. Suburban whites (including the white dope dealers) can breathe a little easier, falsely believing that somebody is really doing something about the problem.

Back in the "hood," it's business as usual. The number of poor folks who use the stuff or the petty crooks who deal in it grow bigger and more desperate, while the blacks who are their victims still walk in fear.

NOTE: Despite the press scare stories on "ghetto drug violence" most of the victims are not two year old babies, or eighty year old grandmothers, but the dealers and the users themselves. The murders usually stem from busted drug deals, competition for markets and disputes over turf.

II

The first press scare stories on drug crazed black males

appeared in the early 1900s. Newspapers fed white fears with bizarre accounts of the criminal exploits of black "cocaine fiends" supposedly on the prowl for white (women) victims. Hamilton Wright, reputedly the State Department's foremost expert on drug abuse in 1910 put the government seal of approval on the fright tales when he testified, "Cocaine is often the direct incentive to the crime of rape by the negroes of the South and other sections of the country." Wright was way ahead of himself. Three years later Georgia state officials released a study conducted at a Georgia State Sanitarium. The officials surveyed more than 2,000 black patients they found three drug addicts. Among the whites there were 142 addicts. The numbers of black and white patients were roughly equal.

Between the World Wars, blacks trekked to the North in big numbers to escape poverty, peonage, segregation and terror. They found no promised land. The North transformed the mostly poor, underemployed and unemployed Southern black men into mostly poor, underemployed and unemployed Northern black men. As more blacks sunk deeper into the morass of poverty, alienation and hopelessness, the number of junkies slowly grew.

The big jump came in the 1980s. The Reagan-Bush assault on job, income, and social service programs, a crumbling educational system and corporate shrinkage dumped more black males on the streets with no where to go. Some chose guns, gangs, crime and drugs. That some was enough. The media quickly got wind of the story and played it big. *Voila!* The drug problem which is an American problem now became a black problem.

The public freaked. A majority of Americans were ready to dump constitutional guarantees of due process and privacy. The consequences came with break neck speed in the form of drug sweeps, random vehicle checks, illegal searches and seizures, evictions from housing projects and apartments. When it came to the ghetto, many civil liberties protections weren't worth the paper they were written on.

III

Between 1986 and 1991, the dope flowed in BOTH the ghettos and suburbs. The number of whites in state prison on drug charges jumped from 16,000 to 30,000. The number of blacks in state prisons on drug charges soared from 65,000 to 80,000. Why were so many in prison? Reagan, Bush, Senators and House members watched TV and read the papers too. From Butte to Peoria, the public demanded action, and the politicians were ready to oblige. Congress passed legislation imposing mandatory sentences for all drug related offenses.

Judges and a few prosecutors balked. They said the government was overreacting and trying to take the legal play from them. The law stood. Predictably, the number of blacks receiving mandatory federal sentences quickly rose from a trickle to a flood. The sentences ranged from ten years to life.

It didn't matter what the circumstances were or how few grams of white powder were involved. If convicted, that's what an offender got. One of them was twenty year old Michael Winrow. He was convicted in 1989 in Los Angeles for selling 5-1/2 ounces of cocaine worth about $100 dollars on the street. Winrow got a life sentence. The case caused a mild stir at the time. Since then, there have been other Winrows and the public has barely stifled a yawn at their predicament. I'm not, nor should any sane person condone what men like Winrow do. Even Winrow didn't condone it. When asked, he shrugged and said all he wanted was a job.

Even if he had a job, and was as pious as a Monk, he still

could have been detained or at least suspected of drug dealing. With the media fanning the flames, black men everywhere, job or no job, profession or no profession, Ph.D. or no D, suddenly found themselves stopped at roadblocks, shaken down on city streets, questioned in department stores and having makes run on them. This was especially galling for members of the new black bourgeoisie. No matter how far their money or status took them from the "hood," much of white America still saw them as hoods.

An example. Joe Morgan was casually chatting on the phone at the Los Angeles airport between flights. Suddenly, Joe found himself body slammed to the floor and tussling with two white undercover cops. They claimed that Morgan fit the Drug Enforcement Administration's "drug courier" profile. Since neither officer was a Cincinnati Reds fan, Mr. Hall of Famer was just another nigger to them. As it turned out, Morgan was a very expensive "nigger." The Los Angeles City Council eventually agreed to pay him $796,000 to settle his lawsuit.

Even though black professionals like Morgan protested, threatened and even won lawsuits, police and prosecutors shot back that this was a war and sometimes the innocent get hurt. Nobody, however, saw middle-class, white executives or professionals in crucifixion-like stances against walls, or leaning with their hands stretched out over the hoods of their expensive Porsches and Benzs.

What about the white dopers? Many of them were shunted to state court where judges still had some say over sentencing. They received less time (if any) in state prison. In New York, state courts extended their *noblesse oblige* to cocaine dealers while stigmatizing crack dealers. Cocaine dealers were more likely to be released on their own recognizance or low bail, and receive a shorter sentence (Remember the four "Ps"—press, public, panic and perceived danger) than crack dealers. You get only one guess who the majority of crack dealers were.

The cruelest joke of all is that none of this has amounted to a hill of beans in the drug war. Federal and state officials have squandered billions of dollars locking up mostly poor black males. Yet the junk still floods into the ghettos, barrios and suburbs. Federal officials desperately search for a winning strategy. It will be tough. By allowing the media to create the fiction that the drug problem is a black problem, they've dug themselves into a deep hole.

There is no real public consensus for spending massive funds on drug treatment and rehabilitation programs or for making the fat cat dealers major law enforcement targets. Most Americans damn sure won't seriously debate the legalizing of some drugs to cut crime. And politicians damn sure haven't seriously tried to loosen the stranglehold the National Rifle Association uses on Congress to bury any legislation that might slow down the virtual open trafficking of guns in the ghettos AND suburbs.

So people wonder what's next. My answer. Watch TV, read the papers and see who still appears in those flattering police poses.

13

The Other Boyz in the Hood

I got to give it to John Singleton. He did what an army of psychologists, sociologists, historians and government bureaucrats couldn't do. Singleton managed to hoodwink Bill Clinton, whites and far too many blacks into believing that the "gangsta" lifestyle was the black life style. It was all there in his film, *Boyz N the Hood*. Young brothers dissed sisters as "bitches" and "hos," called each other "nigger" and "bitch," cussed, fought and shot at each other. Many patrons left the theaters with smirks on their face as they happily told friends, "Ah, we knew all the time that they were like that." We have seen the enemy and it ain't us.

The film critics loved it. (If nothing else, this should have raised warning flags.) They declared that Singleton as the new Orson Welles and rewarded him with an Academy Award nomination. This was quite an accomplishment for a twenty-two year old fellow who, the year before, was sweating final exams in film classes at the University of Southern California.

I understood why many whites loved *Boyz*. I did not understand why blacks loved it. But, they did. Friends, acquaintances and even relatives went nuts over it. Even some who prided themselves on being political sophisticates and who should know better, tossed sanity out the window and heaped praise on Singleton for telling the raw truth about the ghetto. It got so bad that I stopped arguing with folks over the film.

The minute I dared suggest that Singleton presented a parade of one-dimensional, pop ghetto stereotypes, I was shouted down. Even though I have lived and worked in South Central Los Angeles for more than thirty years, before many of my critics were even born, they still told me, "You just don't know how it is with blacks." I hadn't seen blacks get so steamed over an issue since Thomas vs. Hill. Finally, I decided to follow Singleton's advice and keep the peace. I shut-up.

II

Still, I wondered. Were blacks that starved to see themselves on the screen that they accepted uncritically the Singleton/white critic's vision of how young black men behaved? A few trotted out the tired line, "Well, we really don't see ourselves that much on the scream." Baloney! For the past five decades, blacks have sung, danced, postured, swaggered, beat, shot, stabbed and made love to whites on the screen. They have played cops, robbers, presidents, corporate heads, devils, zombies and spacemen. They've done everything anybody could think of in lolly-pop land. The thrill should have been long gone.

I decided that the black love affair with *Boyz* had less to do with the truth about the "hood" than their ignorance of the "hood." Therefore, I thought it appropriate to administer the following test.

NOTE: *I won't make you turn to the back of the book to find the answer. That annoys me, too.*

III

True or False: Most young black males are high school drop-outs?

They aren't. In 1990, nearly eighty percent of African-Americans graduated from high school and nearly thirty percent were enrolled in college (many in historically black colleges). Many young blacks have even crashed the doors and strolled in the stuffy halls of elite private academies. At last count, people of color made up about one-fourth of the enrollment at some of these schools.

Most young black males have higher educational aspirations than young whites. They desire more prestigious positions in business and the professions. This is why, from slavery to freedom, generations of black parents have chanted this Mantra to their sons, "Get an education, boy," Get an eduction, boy. Get an education, boy."

They knew that they had to be two and three times better than whites just to be considered equal (sort of). They've drilled this into their kids' heads and it stuck. Polls always show the same thing. Blacks consider nothing more precious than education.

The bad news is that black males who desperately want degrees are losing ground. Funding cuts, elimination of scholarships, grants and financial assistance, during the Reagan-Bush years decimated the ranks of young black males in colleges. Those fortunate enough to get their degrees will make much less than white, male college graduates. Young black males haven't given up the dream, but it has become tattered.

IV

True or False: Only a small percentage of young black males join gangs?

Even Daryl Gates got this one right. The former, embattled Los Angeles Police Department "Chief," who called the Rodney King beating an "aberration," said that Los Angeles District Attorney, Ira Reiner, went way off the deep end in 1992 when he claimed that half of all young black males in Los Angeles were gang members. Reiner put the number at 150,000. The "Chief" squirmed at the figure not because it made the black community look bad, but because it made his department look bad.

Others also took Reiner to task for "overstating" the numbers. It was no overstatement. A cynic might say that Reiner, locked in a tight race for re-election at the time, waved the report to the media to get panicky white votes. Even if there were no hidden political agenda, the methods used to compile the numbers stunk. Many names were counted several times in the data base.

Many of the kids whose names wound up in the data base wouldn't know the Crips gang from *Our Gang*. Their names were there because police were more interested in colored skins than colored scarfs. Jaywalking, pitching pennies or star gazing, it didn't matter what the pretext. If a young black male was stopped, his name in perpetuity could read, "gang member."

My son's name is probably kicking around somewhere in that computer. He's a twenty year old undergrad majoring in business at California State University, Dominguez Hills. He 's a good student. He minds his own business. He hasn't done drugs, joined a gang or been arrested. Still the police have run more makes on him than Madonna has lewd pictures in her sex book. Whenever he leaves the house, I sweat worrying about his safety. If you're not a black parent with a son under twenty-five, you wouldn't understand.

Computers should not be blamed for turning young black males into potential police line-up candidates. Politicians like Reiner and the press should be. Scare stories and juggled figures on gangs turn the public's justified fear of crime into unjustified hysteria over black crime. They make whites think that any young black man wearing a funny colored shirt, (even some black businessmen wearing ties), baggy pants, earrings and likes rap music is a "gangsta." The fact is neither Reiner nor the press know how many young black males are really in gangs. Gang experts put the figures much lower than they do.

After subtracting the wanna be's and the hanger on's from the total, they say that maybe one in five young black males is a hard core gang member (That's also much too high). The other way is to look at who are the perpetrators and the likely victims of gang violence. Innocent bystanders are not at the greatest risk. Police officials trace less than one in ten victims of violent crime to gangs. Drug experts estimate that black gangs control only a small percentage of the drug trade.

NOTE: Most of the dope dealers are small time, free lance operators out to make a fast buck. The supplies are tightly controlled by drug cartels. The men who pull the strings on import, supply, price, protection and hits live far from the borders of the "hood."

The worst ones to ask for numbers are the gang members

themselves. Some of the "leaders," drunk with their new found celebrity status courtesy of appearances on Geraldo, Oprah, Donohue and *Nightline*, have wildly exaggerated their importance and power. They've been helped along not only by the press, but by some doting black leaders who hail them as Malcolm X's reincarnated. They forget that Big Red was an avid reader in prison. He studied and debated for many years before he became Malcolm X. If many of the gang "leaders" raised a book, it's an act of God. Only a few scant months before Koppel discovered them, many were more concerned with the contents of the pocketbooks of old ladies on the streets of the "hood" than textbooks.

Some of the older gang bangers who have paid their dues doing long stretches in joints throughout the nation have had time to think about the "gangsta" lifestyle. Stanley "Tookie" Williams is one. The reputed Crip co-founder is doing time at San Quentin. He says it's no mystery why some young black males join gangs. "They feel left out in a white dominated society." Tookie did not glamorize the life. Listening to him, you just know that men like him are still a distinct minority in the "hood."

V

True or False: Young black males who join gangs have low self-esteem, are low achievers and are full of self-hate?

Tookie gave the answer away. But let's elaborate. In 1948 psychologist Dr. Kenneth Clark conducted his famous "doll tests" on groups of black kids. He put the children in a room with black and white dolls and observed the ones with which they played. He found that many of them picked the white dolls. Clark wasn't surprised. This demonstrated that the years of segregation, poverty and denial had made black kids feel worthless. White is right, black stay way back. Clark hoped that the test results would persuade the Supreme Court to strike down school segregation in the Brown vs. the Board of Education case.

Sadly, the well-meaning Clark had planted a bad seed. During the 1960s, the sociologists reaped the grim harvest. They followed Clark's lead, conducted their own tests on black children. They concluded that the ghetto was a hopeless muddle of poverty and deviancy. Blacks were hapless, self-hating, ambitionless wastrels. Clark blamed racism. Many sociologists and psychologists blamed blacks. A spate of scholarly articles hammered hard on this theme.

By the 1970s, a few researchers became suspicious. There were just too many blacks chasing careers, diplomas and degrees. Even the ones who weren't, said they'd like to if they had the chance. The researchers backtracked to the original Clark tests. With all due respect to the professor, they suggested that he really hadn't proven that blacks hated themselves. He proved only that: a) They did not play with black dolls because they didn't have them; b) They played with white dolls because they were curious about them; and c) Even then, a significant number of the kids preferred to play with black dolls. When others duplicated the tests years later, and included white kids, they found a sizeable number of black and some white children chose the black dolls for play activity.

NOTE: Since white people and self-hate are oxymorons in American society, nobody would dare accuse them of self-hate or low self-esteem.

These psychologists blew the old theories apart. They found that black high schoolers had greater self-esteem, self-worth and self-initiative than whites. Black children were not mesmerized by everything white. They were more concerned about what their friends, parents and relatives thought about them than white folks did.

If the black child went bad, it wasn't because he thought that he was a miserable wreck of a person. It was because he knew he lived in a miserable wreck of a society that denied him a decent education, job and hope. A twenty-four year old long time member of the Bloods gang in Watts put it simply, "The average black person I know is just like me and can't get a job. Most of us don't have another way of being somebody other than a gang."

In Los Angeles in 1992, Bloods and Crips gang leaders drew up a peace pact. It contained an elaborate economic blueprint for community improvement. It was hailed by many as a marvel of ingenuity, creativity and originality. If they were culturally deprived, social invalids, explain this?

VI

True or False: Black violence is as natural as Apple pie is American?

The truth is that violence is as American as Apple pie. *Time Magazine* paused briefly from reminding us about the "blood scarred streets of South Central Los Angeles" (God, why does that sound like something that some eager beaver writer or more likely a grizzled editor remembered from their high school English literature class?) to do a lengthy feature on teen violence in the suburbs. They noted that the FBI found crime and violence inching up in the suburbs while it dropped in the "hood." In 1993, more suburbanites than ever said they were cringing at the folks in their own neighborhoods.

Does that mean that there's a subculture of violence

germinating in the flowery gardens of white suburbia?

For years, the media and some sociologists speculated that maybe there's something in the genes, air or blood of the ghetto poor that makes young black men commit mayhem and murder. This assumes that at heart the black doctor, lawyer, engineer, plumber or teacher's son is a drive-by shooter or gangbanger. This assumes racism and poverty are mere trifles and that all blacks have a higher tolerance for violence.

Not true. Young men of all colors commit more crimes and are more violence prone. How could it be otherwise? They are fed a steady diet of cops, robber, *Rambo* and *Terminator* macho violence on TV and in the movies at a time when the Testosterone is flowing at record levels in their young bodies. They are taught that fist, knives, guns (and they're everywhere) rather than discourse, discussion and compromise are the honorable way to settle disputes. What message does it send about the value of life when young people watch the body count rise while the adults make pious statements about the "senselessness" of the carnage, and then do virturally nothing to stop it.

The "subculture of violence" theorists sometimes point to the astronomically high number of blacks in prisons and jails to prove that young blacks are habitually violent and dangerous. Not so. In 1991, more than seventy percent of young males arrested were white, twenty-five percent were black. Yet a strange thing happened between arrest and trial. Only thirty-five percent of whites were held in custody while forty-four percent of the blacks were held.

Racism? The experts, say no. They claim that they can't lock up their little Johnnies for shoplifting bubble gum, deflating tires or scrawling "I Love Susie" on walls. Juvenile delinquents, yes, criminals no. They don't peddle dope, gang rape, shoot babies from moving cars or rob grandmothers like the "boyz in the hood." But, a lot of white "boyz" do these things in their "hoods," too.

In 1990, 32,000 more young whites were arrested for murder, forcible rape, robbery and assault than black juveniles. Even so, 300 more blacks were placed in custody and 200 more blacks than whites were tried as adults. A Chicago probation officer tells how they get away it. "When children of the middle and upper class do come to court they often arrive with both parents, community counselors, school representatives bearing report cards and private attorneys representing them." A poor black kid is lucky if his grandmother shows up in court with him.

NOTE: *In December 1993, the nation was shocked by the brutal strangulation murder of twelve year old Polly Klaas. When Richard Allen Davis, a white ex-con, confessed to the murder more than a few wondered how a creature with nearly twenty prior arrests for crimes that included robbery, assault, possession of a dangerous weapon and drug dealing could still be out prowling the streets. As always, they blamed it on the laxity of the criminal justice system. My question: How many black men arrested twenty times for violent crimes would the system be that "lax" with? One more thing. Davis apparently wasn't too fazed about the national howl to crack down on men like him. His attorney said that he was ready to plead guilty if he could receive life imprisonment rather than the death penalty.*

Violence isn't born into young black males. Black males are born into a violent society.

True or False: The culture of poverty breeds violence?

How many dope addicts, dealers, drive-by shooters and muggers do you know that are college graduates, have professions, operate businesses and are active participants in society's institutions? Now, how many blacks does society deny these educational and economic benefits too? The answer is the same as above.

VII

True or False: My wife Barbara holds a Masters degree from the University of Southern California. She is an administrative professional in the University's Real Estate Development Office and a licensed real estate agent. She belongs to several respected civic organizations. She is also a member of the Crips street gang?

I'm not trying to be cutesy. As a lark, if you answered true, you're right. During the course of a staff meeting with other office administrators at her office one afternoon, a white co-worker anxiously mentioned that he had spotted some graffiti on a wall near the university's recently completed townhouse development. The gentleman wondered if the graffiti was the handiwork of gang members.

While he spoke, Barbara, who happened to be the only black in the meeting, noted that he kept his eyes locked on her. She got the distinct impression he was talking to her. She's not a paranoid person. She generally goes out of her way to give people the benefit of the doubt. She's one of the last persons that whites could accuse of being too sensitive about race or of always seeing racism everywhere. Yet she did think it odd that when the subject was gangs the whites looked at her. The rest of the time she was mostly ignored.

I mention this only to show the danger of stereotyping. If most whites, non-blacks and some blacks think that ALL young black males are gang members, it's only a short and dangerous step for them to assume that indeed ALL blacks wear the colors. That's why the young brother from Detroit decked out in gold chains and wearing earrings at the gang peace conference in Kansas City in May 1993, had fun with the media. He told news reporters that he thought the conference was bullshit and that he was going to keep on killing.

The brother walked away with the rest of the reporters tailing him like anxious puppies. Suddenly he turned, laughed and said that he was lying. One of the more astute reporters couldn't resist. He wrote this about the incident, "he sneered as if to say such a sensational account would have been invented by the media regardless of his true words." He was right.

POSTSCRIPT

America's Hidden Agenda Against Black Males

I sometimes forget about how America sees black men. That's why I got excited when Cynthia (not her real name) called to tell me that she had convinced her story editor at National Public Radio to do a Father's Day feature on "three generations of black men." Cynthia who works as a free lance producer for NPR wanted to interview me, my father and my son.

Cynthia assured me that this would not be another crime-drug-gangs-poverty-dereliction story about black men. To get a good family feel, she suggested that she tape us during a family dinner. She would get some ambient sound while we ate and conversed. After dinner, she would do the taping.

Cynthia was very thorough. She spent several hours discussing our family's concerns and achievements. She wanted listeners to feel the warmth and love that we felt for each other.

A few days later, Cynthia called and thanked me. She said that the material was great. A day later, she called again. She told me that her editor decided not to air the program on Father's Day. NPR wanted something a "little lighter." She again assured me that they liked the material. The red flag inched up higher in my mind.

Over the next few weeks, she called several times. She assured me that NPR was still interested but that she was now working with another editor who wanted more background material. Each time I asked her if she had a tentative air date. Cynthia said that NPR rarely gave producers specific air dates for features. Two months, and finally, three editors later, Cynthia assured me that NPR was still interested, but she had another new editor who wanted to refocus the feature. What the hell did that mean? She was vague. I told her that they were jerking her around. She weakly protested that they still wanted to do something.

They probably did. They simply didn't have a clue how to handle a story spotlighting the successes of black men. NPR along with much of the media, had built an impregnable tomb and locked themselves in. If the story is not crime, drugs, gangs or poverty they're lost. Cynthia reluctantly agreed. The story never aired.

II

Shortly after the NPR fiasco, the Anti-Defamation League in 1993 revealed that thirty-one percent of young whites between eighteen and thirty years old thought blacks were lazy and violence prone. The political pundits seemed surprised. I was too. I was surprised the percentage was that low. When young whites read the papers and watch TV news programs do they see regular features on successful, prosperous black business, professional and craft persons, artists and political leaders? Or, do they see black males bent over police cars, sitting in court, prison and juvenile halls? Do they see almost daily photo shots of young black scholars. Or do they see mug like shots of young black males as dope dealers, drive- by shooters and gang bangers?

My guess is that many more young whites secretly believe that blacks are lazy and violence prone. They are just too diplomatic to say it. Some people still consider it impolite to admit that they hate blacks.

Thirty years ago many blacks defied water hoses, police dogs and police billy clubs. They sang, prayed and marched against Jim Crow laws. It was good versus evil. Whites applauded them and called them the "moral conscience" of America. Those days are long gone. The applause has been replaced by fear and hysteria of black men. It's affected everyone. And there's a reason.

The Reagan-Bush administration's slash and burn of social programs was not just mean-spirited. It tapped the huge reservoir of racial know nothingness that has always slinked beneath the surface in American society while legitimizing and elevating racial scapegoating to national policy. In an era of scarcity and declining resources, the search for enemies is ruthless. Blacks are the oldest and most visible enemy. They are the logical target.

If Americans think that black males are inherently stupid, there's no need to build more schools, hire more teachers, provide advanced materials, state of the art equipment and a college prep curriculum for them. If Americans think that black males are gang members, drive-by shooters, and dope dealers, there's no need to spend more on job skills training and entrepreneurial programs for them. If Americans think that black men are absentee or irresponsible fathers, there's no need to overhaul and strengthen welfare and income maintenance programs to insure greater family support systems for them.

If Americans think that black males are chronic alcoholics, druggies and disease risks, there's no need to support a national health care program for the poor and uninsured. If Americans believe that black males are derelict and immoral, presidents and political leaders won't say, "We Shall Overcome," won't propose stronger civil rights laws, increased affirmative action programs and greater civil liberties protections.

If Americans believe that young black males are a menace to society, they will pay for armies of police, fortress-like prisons, repressive laws and shrilly call for sending the National Guard into the ghettos while gutting social programs and bankrupting cities. Many police and public officials in saner moments privately admit that none of this has made a dent in crime or the streets any safer.

But, they can't stop. So blacks are caught in a Catch 22. When they complain, they are told to stop yapping about racism and poverty and start cleaning up their own communities. When sympathetic whites complain, they are told that liberalism is dead or that when they get mugged they'll be talking about "those people," too. When sympathetic Jews complain, they are told that blacks are anti-Semitic. When sympathetic Latinos and Asians, complain they are told to watch out, blacks will take your jobs and burn down your stores. It's victim blaming with a vengeance.

The saddest part of this is that many blacks have swallowed the poison of racism. Many black men don't call black women "sister." They call them "bitches" and "hos." Many black men don't call other black men "brothers." They call them "nigger" and "bitch." Many black women don't call black men "brother" either. They call them "dogs," "animals" and "bastards." Many black women don't call black men "sweetheart" and "lover." They call them "disguised rapists." Many black men don't respect and revere their parents and elders. They demean or terrorize them.

The moment many black men and women have an extra dollar, they head for the furthest suburbs, cross their fingers, and pray that no one burns a cross on their lawn or calls their children "nigger" in the schools. Many black leaders will spend as much time calling for more police, prisons and boot camps as they do calling for jobs, education and health programs. Meanwhile, the brothers and sisters left behind in the ghettos get poorer, angrier and more desperate.

The black unity that many blacks talked and dreamed about during the 1960s has become a fractured nightmare. I can't say that evil men plotted or scripted all this in a backroom. Things never work that way. They don't have to. The assassination of the black male image has transformed black men into universal bogeymen. The trick is to transform them back into universal human beings. If not, writer Charles Carroll who confidently told the world a century ago that the black man was a beast may yet have the last word.

REFERENCE NOTES

Chapter
Page No.

OVERVIEW
The Growth Industry in Black Male Mythology

2   Terry McMillan, *Waiting to Exhale* (New York:
         Pocket Star Books, 1992) 328-329.

2   Michelle Ingrassia, "A World Without Fathers,"
         Newsweek, August 23, 1993, 17-27.

3   Janine Jackson, "Talk Radio Who Gets to Talk,"
         Extra!, April/May, 1993, 14-17.

3   Thomas F. Pettigrew, "New Politics of Racism,"
         Rutgers Law Review #37, Summer, 1985, 685-691.

4   Andrew Billingsley, *Climbing Jacob's Ladder: The
         Enduring Legacy of African-American Families* (New
         York: Simon & Schuster, 1992) 147-169.

4   Sheryl Stolberg and Stephanie Gross, "Gunfire Deaths of Black Teens in Stark Rise," *Los Angeles Times*, June 10, 1992, 1.

5   David Savage, "1 in 4 Young Blacks in Jail or in Court Control," *LAT*, February 27, 1990, 1.

1
The Negro a Beast ... or in the Image of God

7   Eric Lichtblau, "King Discusses Beating with Students," *LAT*, November 19, 1992, 3.

8   *LAT*, November 20, 1992, 1.

8   Richard Bardolph, ed., *The Civil Rights Record, Black America and the Law, 1849-1870* (New York: Thomas Y.Crowell, Co., 1970) 102.

8   —Bardolph, 103-104.

9   Harvey Wish, ed., *Ante-Bellum* (New York: Capricorn Books, 1960) 14, 89.

9   Forrest G. Wood, *The Black Scare: The Racist Response to Emancipation and Reconstruction* (Berkeley: University of California Press, 1968) 1-79.

10   Eric Foner, *Reconstruction* (New York: Harper & Row, 1988).

10   George M. Frederickson. *The Black Image in the White Mind, 1817-1914* (New York: Harper & Row, 1971) 249, 281, 251.

11   —Frederickson, 253.

11   —Bardolph, *The Civil Rights Record,* 107.

12   Rayford Logan, "The Negro as Portrayed in Representative Northern Magazines and Newspapers," in Barry N. Schwartz and Robert Disch, *White Racism* (New York: Dell Publishing, 1970) 395.

12   Upton Sinclair, *The Jungle* (1905 Reprint New American Library, 1964) 270.

12   —Frederickson, *The Black Image* , 260.

13   —Frederickson, 280-281.

13   Seymour L. Gross and John Edward Hardy, *Image of the Negro in American Literature* (Chicago: University of Chicago Press, 1966) 80.

13   Donald Boggle, *Toms, Coons, Mulattos, Mammies and Bucks* (New York: Continuum Publishing Co., 1989) 10, 8.

14   Robert L. Zangrando, *The NAACP Crusade Against Lynching, 1909-1950* (Philadelphia: Temple University, 1980) 6-7.

14   W.E.B. DuBois, "Mob Tactics," *Crisis* #34, August,

1927, 204.

14   —Frederickson, *The Black Image in the White Mind*, 274.

14   *Thirty Years of Lynching, 1889-1918* (New York: NAACP, 1919) 36.

14   *The Works of Theodore Roosevelt, Vol. 17* (New York: Charles Scribners & Sons, 1925) 411-415.

15   Logan, "The Negro as Portrayed in Representative Northern Magazines and Newspapers," 397, 393, 396.

17   "Falling Behind: A Report on How Blacks Have Fared Under Reagan," *Journal of Black Studies* #17, December, 1986, 148-172.

17   Martin A. Lee and Norman Soloman, *Unreliable Sources: A Guide to Detecting Bias in News Media* (New York: Carol Publishing Group, 1990) 238-244.

17   *LAT*, October 31, 1993, 35.

2
The Fine Art of Black Male Bashing

19   Larry Martz, "A Murderous Hoax," *Newsweek*, January 22, 1990, 16-22.

20   Joe Sharkey, *Deadly Greed: The Stuart Murder Case in Boston and the 1980's in America,* (New York: Prentice-Hall Press, 1991) 124, 126, 137, 136.

20   —Sharkey, 144.

21   —Martz, "A Murderous Hoax," 22.

22   David Shaw, "What's the News? White Editors Make the Call," *LAT,* December 13, 1990, 1.

23   David Halberstam, *The Powers That Be* (New York: Alfred A. Knopf, 1979) 62.

23   —Halberstam, 267, 205, 216.

23   —Shaw, "White Editors," *LAT,* December 13, 1990, 1.

24   Ben Bagdikian, *The Media Monopoly* (Boston: Beacon Press, 1990).

24   —Shaw, "Negative News and Little Else," *LAT,* December 11, 1990, 1.

25   *New York Times,* August 25, 1993, B1.

26   Ronald Brownstein, "Clinton, Bush Step Up Debate on Family Values," *LAT,* May 22, 1992, 22.

26   Douglas Jehl, "Quayle Deplores Eroding Values," *LAT,* May 20, 1992, 1.

26   —Ingrassia, "A World Without Fathers," *Newsweek.*

30   Rochelle Sharp, "In Latest Recession Only Blacks
Suffered Net Income Loss," *Wall Street Journal*,
September 14, 1993, 1.

30   Billy J. Tidwell, "A Profile of the Black Unemployed," *State of Black America, 1987* (New York:
Urban League, 1987) 236.

30   "Urban Poverty Expert Talks About Causes," *Los
Angeles Wave*, September 18, 1993, 1.

31   Jeannye Thornton and David Whitman, "Whites'
Myths About Blacks," *U.S. News & World Report*,
November 9, 1992, 41-44.

32   —Sharkey, *Deadly Greed*, 235.

3
From Slavery to the Sports Arena

33   *NYT*, January 16, 1988, 47; *NYT*, January 26, 1988,
II, 8.

34   Frederick Douglass, *Life and Times of Frederick
Douglass* (New York: Collier Books, 1962) 148.

34   Arthur Ashe, Jr., *A Hard Road to Glory: A History of
the Black Athlete, 1619-1918, Vol. 1* (New York:
World Books, 1988) 19-21.

35   Harry Edwards, *The Revolt of the Black Athlete* (New York: The Free Press, 1970).

36   William Oscar Johnson, "The Black Athlete Revisited, " *Sports illustrated*, August 5, 1991, 40.

39   *LAT*, September 17, 1983, VI, 1.

4
Doing the Wrong Thing by Spike

42   Earl Ofari Hutchinson, "Racial Double Standard Puts Spike Lee at a Disadvantage," *LAT*, June 8, 1992, 3.

43   See Daniel J. Leab, *From Sambo to Superspade: The Black Experience in Motion Pictures* (Boston: Houghton-Mifflin, 1975).

44   *Spike Lee's Gotta Have It* (New York: Simon and Schuster, 1987) 316-317.

45   *Habla Malcolm X* (New York: Pathfinder Press, 1993) 108.

5
Thomas, Tyson and Tall Tales

47   *LAT*, November 10, 1993, 1.

47   Ellen Bravo, "Sexual Harassment," *Service Employees Union*, #6 Winter, 1992, 16-17.

48   E.J. Dionne, Jr., "Schism in the Black Community Brought to Bar," *NYT*, July 4, 1991, 1; *Washington Post*, August 9, 1991, 1.

49   —See Boggle, *Toms, Coons, Mulattos, Mammies and Bucks.*

50   Charles Murray, "The Coming White Underclass," *Wall Street Journal*, October 29, 1993, 12.

50   *LAT,* March 26, 1993, 19.

51   Earl Ofari Hutchinson, "Tyson Brought Up Images Black Men Can't Ignore," *Guardian*, March 11, 1992, 18.

51   Jose Torres, *Fear and Fire* (New York: New American Library, 1989).

51   Kweku Hanson, "Racial Disparities and the Law of Death: The Case for a New Hard Look at Race-Based Challenges to Capital Punishment," *National Black Law Journal* #2, 1990, 299-302.

51   Hugo A. Bedeau, *Capital Punishment in the United States* (New York: Oxford University Press, 1982) 107-119.

52   *NYT*, August 13, 1991, 31.

52   Bill Turque, "Judgment for the Wilders," *Newsweek*, August 27, 1990, 30.

53   *The Complete Works of Shakespeare* (New York: Avenal Books, 1975) 1114.

53   —Jordan, *White Over Black*, 156.

54   —Frederickson, *The Black Image in the White Mind*, 278-279.

54   Winthrop D. Jordan, *White Over Black: American Attitudes Toward the Negro, 1550-1812* (Baltimore: Penguin Books, 1968) 159.

55   U.S. Department of Commerce, *Statistical Abstract of the United States, 1982-1983*, (Washington: GPO, 1984) 195.

55   *Dallas Times Herald*, August 19, 1990, 20.

55   Michael L. Radelet, "Executions of Whites for Crimes Against Blacks: Exceptions to the Rule?" *The Sociological Quarterly* #30, 1989, 529-544.

56   "Interview with Robert Johnson," *Jet*, September 29, 1993, 56.

57   Gerda Lerner, ed. *Black Women in White America* (New York: Pantheon Books, 1972) 216.

57   William Oliver, "Sexual Conquests and Patterns of Black-on-Black Violence: A Structural-Cultural Perspective," *Violence and Victims* #4, 1989, 257-273.

58   John Hope Franklin, *From Slavery to Freedom* (New York: Random House, 1969) 573-622.

59   Audrey Edwards, "Survey Report," *Black Enterprise*, August, 1990, 95.

59   Black Scholar, ed. *Court of Appeal: The Black Community Speaks Out on the Racial and Sexual Politics of Thomas vs. Hill* (New York: Ballantine Books, 1992).

59   "National Survey of Black Americans, 1979-1980," in Billingsley, *Climbing Jacob's Ladder*, 225.

6
Ain't I a Nigger Too

63   See Winthrop D. Jordan's, *White Over Black: American Attitudes Toward the Negro, 1550-1812* .

64   The Complete Works of William Shakespeare, 1147.

64   Jordan, *White Over Black*, 70.

64   Gilbert Osofsky, *The Burden of Race* (New York: Harper & Row, 1967) 78.

64   Mark Twain, *The Adventures of Huckleberry Finn*, 174-175.

65   Gene Marine, "I've Got Nothing Against The

Colored, Understand," in *White Racism*, 227.

65   David Garrow, *Bearing the Cross* (New York: William Morrow, 1986) 475-525.

65   Logan, "The Negro as Portrayed in Representative Northern Magazines and Newspapers," 395-398.

65   W.E.B. DuBois, "That Capital "N," *Crisis* #11, February, 1916, 184.

66   Zangrando, *The NAACP and the Anti-Lynching Crusade*, 6-7.

66   Edward K. Weaver, "Racial Sensitivity Among Negro Children," in *White Racism*, 183.

67   *LAT*, August 6, 1993, 1, Davies' Quote.

67   Miles Corwin, "A Jail Without Walls," *LAT*, October 13, 1993, B1.

68   Richard Wright, *Uncle Tom's Children* (New York: Harper & Row, 1965) 9-10.

7
The Way Things Ought *Not* To Be

69   Rush Limbaugh, *The Way Things Ought To Be*, (New York: Simon and Schuster, 1992) 325.

69   Claudette E. Bennett, "The Black Population in the United States, March 1990 and 1989," *Department of*

Commerce, U.S. Census (Washington : GPO, 1991) 7.

70   Carl Ginsberg, *Race and Media: The Enduring Life of the Moynihan Report* (New York: Institute for Media Analysis, 1989).

71   Andrew Billingsley, "Understanding African-American Family Diversity," in *State of Black America, 1990* (New York: Urban League, 1990) 101.

72   James Risen, "History May Judge Reagonomics Very Harshly," *LAT*, November 8, 1992 D1.

72   Department of Commerce, *America's Black Population 1970-1982* (Washington: GPO, 1984) 16-17.

72   Marilyn French, *The War Against Women* (New York: Summitt Books, 1992) 185.

72   Doris R. Entswisle and Karl L. Alexander, "Summer Setback: Race, Poverty, School Composition and Mathematics Achievements in the First Two Years of School," *American Sociological Review* #57, February, 1992, 72-84.

72   Bruce A. Chadwick and Tim B. Heaton, *Statistical Handbook on the American Family* (New York: Onyx Press, 1992).

73   David Halberstam, *the Fifties* (New York: Villard Books, 1993) 508-520.

74   Limbaugh, *The Way Things Ought To Be*, 431, 434.

75   Billingsley, *Climbing Jacob's Ladder*, 207.

8
Minister Farrakhan or Adolph Farrakhan?

78   *LAT*, September 11, B1; September12, B1; September 16, 1985, B5.

79   *LAT*, October 10, 1993, B3.

9
Why Are They Waiting to Exhale?

81   Shahrazad Ali, *The Black Man's Guide to Understanding the Black Woman* (Philadelphia: Civilized Press, 1989).

83   Michele Wallace, *Black Macho and the Myth of the Superwoman* (New York: Dial Press, 1978).

83   Ntozake Shange, *For Colored Girls Who Have Considered Suicide/When the Rainbow Is Enuf* (New York: Collier Books, 1977).

84   Gloria Naylor, *The Women of Brewster Place* (New York: Viking Press, 1982).

84   Alice Walker, *The Color Purple* (New York: Pocket Books, 1982).

84   Pearl Cleage, *Deals with the Devil And Other Reasons*

to Riot (New York: Ballantine Books, 1993) 153.

85   bell hooks, *Ain't I A Woman* (Boston: South End Press, 1981) 88-90.

85   Frederick Engels, *The Origin of the Family, Private Property And The State* (Moscow: Foreign Languages Publishing House, 1960) 120-136.

86   —hooks, *Ain't I A Woman*, 94.

86   Andrew Billingsley, *Black Families in White America* (Englewood Cliffs, N.J.:Prentice-Hall, 1968) 38-48.

86   Eugene Hillman, *Polygamy Reconsidered: African Plural Marriage* (Maryknoll, N.Y.: Orbis Books, 1975) 43-44.

87   —Billingsley, *Climbing Jacob's Ladder*, 94-95, 240-243.

87   Herbert Gutman provides solid evidence that for nearly a century following emancipation there were marked differences in the domestic patterns of black and white familes, *The Black Family in Slavery and Freedom, 1750-1925* (New York: Random House, 1975) 363-460.

87   —hooks, *Talking back, thinking feminist, thinking black* (Boston: South End Press, 1989) 155.

88   See McMillan, *Waiting to Exhale* .

89   Amy Tan, *The Joy Luck Club* (New York: G.P Putnam, 1989).

89   Isabel Allende, *Eva Luna* (Barcelona: Plaza & Janes Editores, 1991).

91   —Billingsley, *Climbing Jacob's Ladder*, 245-261, 243.

92   Earl Ofari Hutchinson, *Black Fatherhood: The Guide to Male Parenting* (Los Angeles: Middle Passage Press, 1992).

10
No Thriller for Michael Jackson

93   Sonia Nazario and Amy Wallace, "International Furor Stirred by Allegations on Jackson," *LAT*, August 26, 1993, 1.

95   *Nation*, October 11, 1993, 376.

95   *LAT*, September 19, 1993, 1.

96   Robert Joseph Taylor, Linda M. Chatters, M. Belinda Tucker and Edith Lewis, "Developments in Research on Black Families," *Journal of Marriage and the Family* #52, November, 1990, 993-1014.

11
What's Love Got To Do With It? More Than You Think

97   Tina Turner, *I, Tina* (New York: William Morrow, 1986) 206-207.

98   Audrey Edwards, "What Becomes a Sex Goddess Most," *Essence*, July, 1993, 52.

99   —Turner, *I, Tina*, 154.

100   Leonard Berkowitz, "The Study of Urban Violence," *American Behavioral Scientist* #11, March-April, 1968, 14-17.

12
The War on Drugs *IS* a War on Black Males

103   Ron Harris, "Blacks Feel Brunt of Drug War," *LAT*, April 22, 1990, 1.

103   Sam Vincent, "Is The Drug War Racist?" *USA Today*, July 23-25, 1993, 1.

104   Margo Walker, "Black Students Just Say No," *Emerge*, August, 1991, 4.

104   Jeanette Covington, "Self-Esteem and Deviance: The Effects of Race and Gender," *Criminology* #24, November, 1986, 105-138.

104   Kirk A. Johnson, "Objective News and Other Myths: The Poisoning of Young Black Minds," *Journal of Negro History* #60, 1991, 332.

105   Lionel McPherson, "News Media, Racism and the Drug War," *Extra!*, April 5, 1992, 5.

105   Linda S. Wong and Bruce K. Alexander, "Cocaine-Related Deaths: Media Coverage in the War on Drugs," *The Journal of Drug Issues* #21, 1991, 105-119.

105   Beny J. Primm, "Drug Use: Special Implications for Black America," in *State of Black America, 1987* (New York: Urban League, 1987) 147.

106   Randolph N. Stone, "The War on Drugs: The Wrong Enemy and the Wrong Battlefield," *National Bar Association Magazine*, December, 1989, 18-35.

107   —Vincent, "Is the Drug War Racist?" 1.

107   Jim Newton, "Judges Voice Anger Over Mandatory U.S. Sentencing," *LAT*, August 21, 1993, 1.

107   *LAT*, April 22, 1990, 1.

108   Mark Whitaker, "A Crisis of Shattered Dreams," *Newsweek*, May 6, 1991, 28-31.

108   Victor Merina, "Joe Morgan Suit Protests Drug Profile," *LAT*, August 7, 1990, B1.

108   *LAT*, November, 17, 1993, 1.

108   Steven Belenko, Jeffrey Fagan and Ko-Lin Chin, "Criminal Justice Response to Crack," *Journal of*

Research in Crime and Delinquency," #28, February 1991, 55-74.

13
The Other Boyz in the Hood

113   Claudette E. Bennett, "The Black Population in the United States, March 1989 and March 1990," *Department of Commerce, U.S. Census,* Table B, 3.

113   Sylvester Monroe, "Diversity Comes to Elite Prep Schools," *Emerge,* August, 1993, 50-54.

113   Michael Hughes and David Demo, "Self-perceptions of Black Americans: Self-Esteem and Personal Efficacy," *American Journal of Sociology* #95, July, 1989, 132-159.

113   Bennet Harrison, "For Blacks a Degree Doesn't Automatically Mean Higher Incomes," *LAT,* September 2, 1990, M4.

114   Sheryl Stolberg, "150,000 Are in Gangs, Report by D.A. Claims," *LAT,* May 22, 1992, 1.

114   Rosalind X. Moore, "L.A. Police Hang 'Gang Banger' Label on City's Young Black Males," *Final Call,* June 15, 1992, 2.

115   John A. Backstrand, Don C. Gibbons and Joseph F. Jones, "Who is in Jail," *Crime & Delinquency* #38, April, 1992, 219-229.

115 Jack Katz, "Gangs Aren't the Cause of Crime," *LAT*, May 31, 1992, B5.

115 Steven H. Stumpf, *Conference Report*, "Crack: Crisis in the African-American Community," April 3, 1990.

116 Barbara Cottman Becnel, "Interview with Stanley (Tookie) Williams," *LAT*, August 22, 1993, M3.

116 Kenneth Clark and Mamie Clark, *Racial Identification and Preferences in Negro Children* (New York: Holt, 1947).

116 Darlene Powell Hopson and Derek S. Hopson, "Implications of Doll Color Preferences Among Black Preschool Children and White Preschool Children," *Journal of Black Psychology*, #14, February, 1988, 57-63.

117 Michael McMillan, "The Doll Test Studies: From Cabbage Patch to self-Concept, *JBP*, #14, February, 1988, 69-72.

117 Kathryn P. Johnsen and Morris L. Medley, "Academic Self-Concept Among Black High School Seniors: An Examination of Perceived Agreement with Selected Others," *Phylon*, #39, 1978, 264-274.

118 Andrea Ford and Carla Rivera, "Hope Takes Hold as Bloods, Crips Say Truce is for Real," *LAT*, May 21, 1992.

118   Jill Smolowe, "Danger in the Safety Zone," *Time,* August 23, 1993, 29.

118   J. Michael Kennedy, "Students Armed and Dangerous," *LAT*, October 10, 1991, 1.

119   See the issues of *National Coalition on Television Violence News*, 1990-1991.

119   Carolyn A. Stroman, "Television's Role in the Socialization of African-American Children and Adolescents," *Journal of Negro History*, #60, 1991, 315-318.

119   Marvin Wolfgang and Franco Ferracuti, *The Subculture of Violence* (London: Tavstock Publications, 1967).

119   Ron Harris, "Hand of Punishment Weighs Heavily on Black Youth," *LAT*, August 24, 1993, 1.

120   Robert Nash Parker, "Poverty, Subculture of Violence and Type of Homicide," *Social Forces*, #19, December 1989, 980-1007.

120   Ronald L. Simons and Phyllis A. Gray, "Perceived Blocked Opportunity as an Explanation of Delinquency Among Lower-Class Black Males: A Research Note," *Journal of Research in Crime and Delinquency*, #26, February, 1989, 90-101.

122   Jesse Katz, "Summit of Gangs Takes Aim at Peace,"
       LAT, May 2, 1993, 1.

POSTSCRIPT
America's Hidden Agenda Against Black Males

124   "New Report Reveals Young Whites Are More
       Biased Against Blacks Than Older Whites Are," *Jet*,
       July 5, 1993, 26-29.

125   Bob Baker, "Stereotypes That Won't Go Away,"
       LAT, May 31, 1992, 1.

125   "Crime: A Conspiracy of Silence," *Newsweek*, May
       18, 1992, 37.

125   Marc Mauer, "Americans Behind Bars," *Criminal
       Justice*, #6, Winter, 1992, 12-18.

126   Joe R. Feagin, "The Continuing Significance of
       Race: Anti-Black Discrimination in Public Places,"
       American Sociological Review #56, 1991, 101-116.

INDEX